CW00363110

LITTLE BOOK OF

ANCIENT EGYPT

Ian Mackenzie

LITTLE BOOK OF
ANCIENT EGYPT

First published in the UK in 2014

© Demand Media Limited 2014

www.demand-media.co.uk

All rights reserved. No part of this work may be reproduced or utilised in any form or by any means, electronic or mechanical, including photocopying, recording or by any information storage and retrieval system, without prior written permission of the publisher.

Printed and bound in Europe

ISBN 978-1-910270-13-4

The views in this book are those of the author but they are general views only and readers are urged to consult the relevant and qualified specialist for individual advice in particular situations.

Demand Media Limited hereby exclude all liability to the extent permitted by law of any errors or omissions in this book and for any loss, damage or expense (whether direct or indirect) suffered by a third party relying on any information contained in this book.

All our best endeavours have been made to secure copyright clearance for every photograph used but in the event of any copyright owner being overlooked please address correspondence to Demand Media Limited, Waterside Chambers, Bridge Barn Lane, Woking, Surrey, GU21 6NL.

CONTENTS

INTRODUCTION

With Egypt's dry climate and lack of encroaching vegetation, buildings and artefacts dating back five thousand years have survived remarkably well. Together with writings from the Greek and Biblical era and the ongoing translations of hieroglyphs carved in stone, these have provided us with a surprisingly detailed and accurate picture of life in ancient Egypt.

The developed culture and sophistication of Egyptian society sprung, seemingly instantly, from a race of desert nomads, never fails to astound. Egyptian civilisation was one of the greatest in the ancient world as well as being one of the longest, lasting for over 3,000 years. The popular image of ancient Egypt is well presented by such wonders as the pyramids, the giant Sphinx at Giza and well preserved funerary treasures but in this introductory book to ancient Egypt we shall explain more about the people responsible for those wonders.

Ancient Egypt's early success derived from its ability to harness the resources of the Nile Valley. The predictable annual flooding and controlled irrigation of the fertile valley provided surplus crops which supported a growing population and developing culture. With resources to spare it was possible to exploit minerals in the valley and surrounding desert, establish trade with surrounding regions and develop a military force capable of defeating foreign enemies. Relying on an independent writing system these activities were organised and controlled by a bureaucracy

ABOVE The Sphinx and pyramids of Giza, instantly recognisable images of Ancient Egypt

of elite scribes, religious leaders and administrators under the ultimate control of a pharaoh.

The Pharaohs, heading Egypt's elaborate system of religious beliefs, were god-kings on earth who at death became gods in their own right. They held the power of life and death in their hands and could command phenomenal resources as demonstrated by the building of pyramids, enormous temples and huge desert statues. But at the time their role as divine deities was regarded with a sort of pragmatic cynicism, as evidenced by the existence of grave robbers, undeterred by tomb curses, and the ease with which the names of pharaohs who offended convention, such as Akhenaten and Queen Hatshepsut, could be expunged from the historical records.

ABOVE The Sphinx and pyramids of Giza, instantly recognisable images of Ancient Egypt

RIGHT Wooden bust of Tutankhamun, the boy-king

The Egyptians kept scrupulous records of the lives of their pharaohs and today scholars still refer to the system of over 30 pharaonic dynasties established by the Egyptian priest Manetho in the third century BC. By convention historians have organised these dynasties into distinct eras, The Old Kingdom, Middle Kingdom and New Kingdom, periods of extreme stability sometimes lasting up to half a millennium, interspersed with shorter eras of relative chaos referred to as the Intermediate Periods. Structured around the conventional chronology of eras and dynasties this book provides a useful reference by listing all the pharaohs in each dynasty and the current best estimate of their dates of rule, including, in the 18th Dynasty, Tutankhamun.

Though a relatively minor Pharaoh, Tutankhamun's appeal is very clear. When discovered by Howard Carter in 1922 his tomb was the only one dating from Egypt's New Kingdom (circa 1550 – 1069 BC) to be found substantially intact, its stone sarcophagus and rich treasure of grave goods unseen since the tomb had been sealed over three thousand years earlier.

And linked with the appeal of the fabulous artefacts is that frisson of horror generated by the Mummy's Curse, supposedly engraved on the outside of the tomb:

"Death Shall Come on Swift Wings To Him Who Disturbs the Peace of the King"

Though the idea of a Curse has proved an excellent muse for any number of mummy themed horror movies, our chapter on Tutankhamun will show that deaths supposedly related to the Curse were largely inventions whipped up by newspapers in the 1920s and 30s simply to boost their sales.

Egyptian civilisation did not end with a bang or sudden defeat by enemies. Instead it petered out slowly in a series of alliances made with later civilisations such as the Greeks and Persians before its final stage as a sort of autonomous colony of the Roman Empire.

Egypt and its ancient civilisation is still a fruitful resource for archaeologists and historians with new discoveries made every year, in museums, laboratories and field excavations. Our last chapter in this Little Book will feature some of the latest discoveries, including secrets revealed by the latest examinations of mummies and the spectacular discovery of the port of Heracleion, sunk in an earthquake around 700 AD.

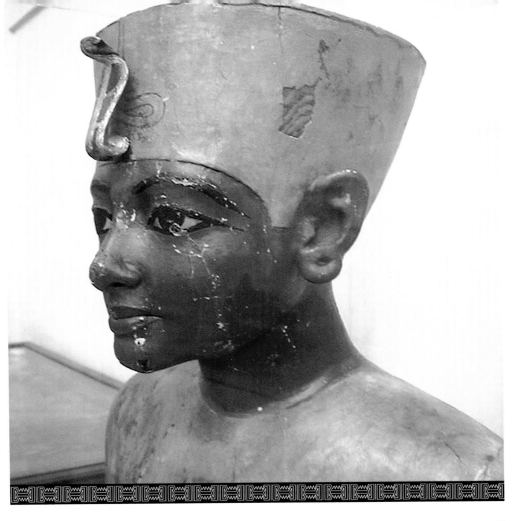

THE ERAS AND DYNASTIES OF ANCIENT EGYPT

Period	Period dates BC	Dynasties	Dynasty dates BC
Pre-Dynastic	Before 3050	0	3150 - 3050
Early Dynastic	3050 - 2686	1	3050 - 2890
		2	2890 - 2686
Old Kingdom	2686 - 2181	3	2686 - 2683
		4	2613 - 2498
		5	2498 - 2345
		6	2345 - 2181
First Intermediate	2181 - 2040	7	2181 -
		8	- 2161
		9	2160 -
		10	- 2040

Period	Period dates BC	Dynasties	Dynasty dates BC
Middle Kingdom	2040 - 1782	11	2040 - 1991
		12	1991 - 1782
Second Intermediate	1782 - 1570	13	1782 - 1650
		14	
		15	1663 -
		16	- 1555
Thebes		17	1663 - 1570
New Kingdom	1549 - 1069	18	1570 - 1293
		19	1293 - 1185
		20	1185 - 1069
		High Priests at Thebes	1080 - 945
Third Intermediate	1069 - 525	21	1069 - 945
		22	945 - 712
		23	818 - 712
		24	727 - 715
		25	747 - 656
		26	664 - 625
Late Period	672 - 332	27	525 - 404
		28	404 - 399
		29	399 - 380
		30	380 - 343
		31	343 - 332
Macedonian Kings			332 - 305
Ptolemaic Dynasty			305 - 30

GLOSSARY

RIGHT An example of a sacred monument, called the 'benben'

Akh - The immortal and unchangeable aspect of a person joining the gods in the underworld after death

Ankh - A symbol of life presented as a looped cross

Ba - An individual's personality, entering the body at birth and leaving at death

Benben - A stone resembling a pyramid and representative of a sun ray

Canopic jars - Four jars used to store the preserved internal organs of mummies

Cartonnage - Papyrus or linen soaked in plaster, shaped around a body and used for mummy masks and coffins

Cartouche - An upright oval lozenge with a horizontal bar at the bottom in which king's names are written

Cenotaph - From the Greek meaning "empty tomb", a tomb built for ceremonial purposes but never intended to be used

Colossus - A larger than life statue of gods, kings and important people such as priests and viziers

Deshret - The Egyptian Red Crown that represented Lower (northern) Egypt

Dromos - A straight, paved avenue flanked by sphinxes

Faience - A glazed material, with a base of either carved soapstone or moulded clay, with an overlay of blue/green colored glass

False door - A door carved or painted on a wall. The ka would use this door to partake of funerary offerings

Hedjet - The White Crown of Lower (southern) Egypt

Hieroglyph - The Egyptian picture language, from the Greek word meaning "sacred carving"

Horus - The falcon headed god Horus was so important to the state religion that Pharaohs were considered his human manifestation and even took on the name Horus

Hypostyle Hall - From Greek and meaning "bearing pillars", this word describes the pillars in the outermost walls of temples that are believed to represent a grove of trees

Ibu - The tent of purification, the place where mummification was performed

Ka - Crafted on the potter's wheel of the god Khnum at the same time of birth, Ka is what we would best describe as a person's soul

Ma'at - The concept of order, truth, regularity and justice which was all important to the ancient Egyptians and personified by the goddess Ma'at

ABOVE Sphinxes of dromos, Karnak temple of Amun-Ra, Egypt

Mastaba - The style of tombs of the early Dynastic and Old Kingdom periods, from the Arabic word for "bench" which accurately describes their rectangular shape

Mummy - From the Persian word "moumiya", a mummy is a corpse dried and preserved by natural or artificial means

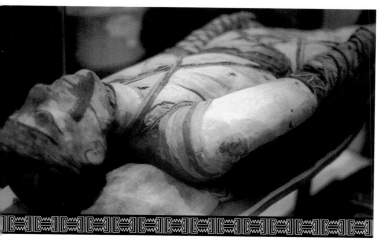

BELOW Egyptian Mummy at the British Museum in London

which was considered a divine metal

Nemes - Striped head cloth worn by the pharaohs

Nilometer - A staircase descending into the Nile and marked with levels above low water for measuring and in some cases recording inundation levels

Nomarchs - Nobles and rulers of the regional nomes

Nomes - Administrative regions of Egypt numbered from the First Cataract in the south to the Delta in the north

Obelisk - A monumental tapering shaft usually topped with a pyramidion

Osirid pillar - A pillar in an open court or portico with a colossal statue of a king forming its front part

Naos - Shrine in which divine statues were kept, usually in a temple sanctuary

Nebu - The Egyptian word for gold

Papyrus - The main Egyptian writing material made by cutting the stem of the papyrus plants into strips, soaking in water to remove sugar and starch and then beating to glue the strips together to form a sheet

Propylon - Gateway that stands in front of a pylon

Pylon - The monumental entrance of a temple, from the Greek word meaning "gate"

Pyramidion - Capstone of a pyramid or the top of an obelisk and sometimes called a Benben stone or primordial mound

Saff tomb - An Arabic word meaning "row" that describes the rock-cut tombs of the early 11th Dynasty that consisted of a row of openings on the hillside

Sarcophagus - Derived from the Greek word meaning "flesh eater", sarcophagus is the stone container within which the coffin and mummy were placed

Scarab - To the ancient Egyptians this dung rolling beetle was sacred as a symbol of regeneration and spontaneous creation because it seemed to emerge from nowhere

Sphinx - A figure with the body of a lion and the head of a man, hawk or a ram

Stele - A stone slab or wooden board decorated or inscribed with paintings, relief or texts. They usually celebrated an event or delivered a proclamation

Was sceptre - This was carried by deities as a symbol of their power and dominion which Kings and, later, people of lower stature are portrayed carrying in mortuary scenes

Wabet - A place where part of the purification and mummification rites were performed

ABOVE Stele in Nectanebo court, Luxor Temple, Egypt

NAMING THE PHARAOHS

RIGHT Serekh
containing the name
of Djet and an
association with
Wadjet, on display
at the Louvre

From the First Dynasty onwards pharaohs were named under a fixed convention known as the royal titular which by the time of the Middle Kingdom embraced five separate names, a format that existed from then through to the end of the Ancient Egyptian civilisation.

Horus name

Originating in the Predynastic Period the Horus name is the oldest form of the pharaoh's name and the oldest known pharaohs are known only by this title, which confirmed the pharaoh's status as the earthly embodiment of the god Horus.

The hieroglyph of the Horus name was written inside a serekh, a stylised representation of a palace façade, together with the falcon image of the god Horus.

Nebty ("two ladies") name

The Nebty name, literally two ladies, was associated with the so-called "heraldic goddesses" of Upper and Lower Egypt: Nekhbet, patron deity of Upper Egypt represented by a vulture and Wadjet, patron deity of Lower Egypt represented by a cobra.

The first known use of a Nebty name was by the First Dynasty pharaoh Semerkhetit but it was not until the Twelfth Dynasty that it was fully established as part of the pharaoh naming convention.

Horus of Gold

Known also as the Golden Horus Name this form of the pharaoh's name typically featured the image of the Horus falcon perched above or beside the hieroglyph for gold.

Egyptologists are uncertain about the meaning of this particular title though one explanation is that it represents the triumph of Horus over his uncle Seth and the symbol for gold implies that "Horus was superior to his foes". In the ancient Egyptian mind gold, which never corrodes, was associated with eternity so perhaps it was intended to convey the pharaoh's eternal Horus name.

Throne name

The pharaoh's throne name was the first of the two names written inside a cartouche and normally accompanied the title nesu-bity, meaning "King of Upper and Lower Egypt".

The throne name came to prominence by the end of the Third Dynasty and would eventually become the most important official title of the pharaoh.

Personal name

Personal name was the name given at birth. When written, the name was preceded by the title "Son of Ra", represented by the hieroglyph of a duck adjacent to an image of the sun, the hieroglyph for Ra, the chief solar deity.

This is the name that modern historians generally use when referring to the kings of Ancient Egypt, using Roman numerals to distinguish between pharaohs with the same name.

Chapter 1

SOURCES AND EVIDENCE

RIGHT The Rosetta Stone, currently in the British Museum

Manetho, Egyptian priest and scholar

The most important source of information about ancient Egypt is the work of Manetho, an Egyptian priest in the Temple of Ra at Heliopolis. As a priest he would have had the skills to read hieroglyphic texts and have access to various temple archives. Of the six or seven works credited to Manetho the most important is his *Aegyptiaca* (*Egyptian History*), sometimes referred to as *Notes about Egypt*.

The term dynasty was coined by Manetho in *Aegyptiaca*, derived from the Greek *dynasteia* which refers to the rule of government. In *Aegyptiaca* he divided pharaonic history into 30 or so different dynasties, identified not just by bloodline but also according to periods of rule from a particular capital or region. Manetho's dynasties established the framework for the study of Ancient Egypt's history that has remained fundamental right up to the present day.

Though dedicated to the pharaoh Ptolemy II Philadelphus (285 – 246 BC) it is likely that the book was written during the reign of his predecessor Ptolemy I Soter (305 – 285 BC). Written in Greek it is likely, too, that the book was prepared as either an alternative or supplementary text to an Egyptian history written a century earlier by the Greek scholar Herodotus. With access to temple records, inscriptions and king-lists dating back to the Predynastic era there is no doubt that *Aegyptiaca* would have been extremely accurate. Unfortunately no copies of the work have survived and we have to rely, instead, on fragments of *Aegyptiaca* reproduced in the works of later scholars such as Josephus (c. 1st century AD), Sextus Julius Africanus (c.AD 220) and Bishop Eusebius (c.400 AD). Personal opinion, political and racial prejudices mean that the fragments of Manetho borrowed by these writers are often contradictory.

For corroboration of Manetho historians have had to scour alternative sources, ideally original written sources from preserved tablets, hieroglyphic inscriptions and surviving papyri.

Evidence from hieroglyphic inscriptions

Hieroglyphic inscriptions providing details of Egyptian life and history survive from the Predynastic era through to AD 394 with reputedly the last recorded inscription on the Temple of Philae. Seemingly after that date the "key" and skill required to read hieroglyphs was lost though during the European Renaissance scholars made some bold and credible attempts at translation. This included the correct identification in 1761 by Abbe Jean Jacques Barthelemy that the oval rings containing a number of

ABOVE Fragment of Palermo Stone at the Petrie Museum, London

building material in the construction of Fort Julien, near Rashid at the Rosetta mouth of the Nile Delta. It was identified and rediscovered by a French Officer of engineers, Lieutenant P.F.X.Bouchard, serving with the Napoleonic Expedition in Egypt.

Inscribed in three scripts representing two languages, each containing the same information, the Rosetta Stone provided a vital key to the translation of hieroglyphs. The upper portion of the stone is written in hieroglyphs, the middle section in Egyptian written script, known as demotic script and typically used for writing on papyrus, while the lower section is in Greek. Working from the Greek, French scholar Jean Francois Champellion was able to "crack the code" of the hieroglyphs and identify the inscription as the Decree of Memphis, a decree of Ptolemy V, dated to the ninth year of his reign, 196BC.

Working with the Stone, Champollion was able confirm the theory that the cartouches did contain the names of royal families and eventually in 1822 produce his lifetime opus, *Lettre a M. Dacier*, an academic paper which immediately enabled the decipherment of hieroglyphs still in situ on preserved buildings or discovered in later excavations.

hieroglyphic signs, what we now know as cartouches, enclosed royal names.

The sesame moment for translating hieroglyphs was the discovery of the Rosetta Stone in 1799. Presumably once part of a temple it had been recycled as

The Palermo Stone, less well known than the iconic Rosetta Stone, was discovered as broken fragments in 1866, but is probably more important as it dates back to the 5th Dynasty (2498 – 2345 BC) and is inscribed on both sides with details of pharaohs from the Predynastic era before 3150 BC through to Neferirkare in the middle of the 5th Dynasty. Inscribed on black diorite the largest fragment of the Palermo Stone is in the Palermo Museum, Palermo while smaller fragments can be seen in Cairo Museum and Petrie Museum, University College London. It is generally assumed to be one of the sources Manetho relied on when compiling his *Aegyptiaca*.

Another important inscribed stone is the Royal List of Karnak, now in the Louvre and providing a list of kings from the first Predynastic king down to Tuthmosis III (1504 – 1450 BC) in the New Kingdom 18th Dynasty.

Still *in situ* on the walls of a corridor in the Hall of Ancestors in the temple of Seti I is the Royal List of Abydon. This portrays Seti with his young son (later Ramesses II) presenting in two rows a list of 76 cartouches of 76 kings from the first king to Seti I. It omits kings of the Second Intermediate Period as well as those deemed pariahs because of their association with Akhenaten's Amarna heresy but scholars have been able to fill in the gaps from the Royal List of Karnak.

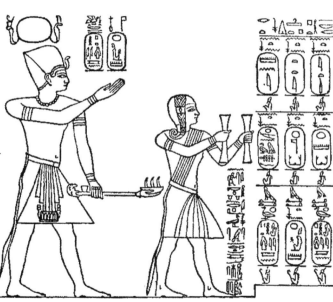

BELOW The start of the Abydos king list showing Seti and his son Ramesses II

BELOW Drawing of
fragments from the
Royal Canon of Turin

A badly damaged duplicate of this list, arranged in three instead of two rows, was removed from the nearby temple of Ramesses II and is now held in the British Museum.

The final important list inscribed on stone is the Royal List of Saqqara, now kept in the Cairo Museum. Damaged and incomplete it was found in the tomb of the Royal Scribe Thunery at Saqqara and displays 47 out of an original 58 cartouches. These list pharaohs from Anedjib of the 1st Dynasty to Ramesses II but omitting, like the Royal List of Abydon, the kings of the second Intermediate Period.

Evidence from papyrus, the Royal Canon of Turin

The most reliable chronological record of the Egyptian kings should have been a papyrus now in the Museum of Turin and referred to as the Royal Canon of Turin. Dated to around 1200BC it originally listed over 300 kings, starting with the

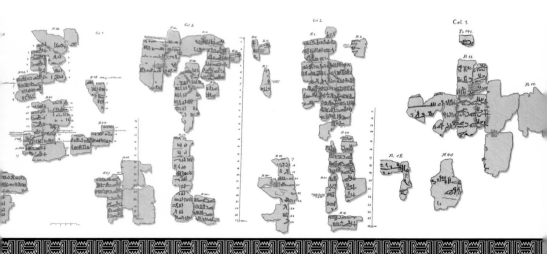

dynasties of Gods followed by the earthly Pharaohs. Originally owned by the king of Sardinia it was badly packed and severely damaged on transhipment to Turin so that what should have been a prime historical source is now just a nightmare jigsaw for scholars of Ancient Egypt.

The few legible fragments that can be read have proved useful as they provide exacts lengths of individual pharaohs' reigns in years, months and days.

Accurate dating

Fixing the absolute historic dates for the rule of individual pharaohs is very difficult. A lot of data is available from the existing resources and though this provides the length of individual reigns accurately and the correct relative order of pharaohs, there are few markers to allow fixed dates to be established.

The best way of fixing dates is by reference to known astronomical events that have been recorded in the ancient Egyptian records, such as the heliacal rising of Sirius, the Dog Star, that moment when it first briefly appears on the eastern horizon at sunset following a period when it has not been visible. We know, for example, that there was a heliacal rising of

Sirius in 1872BC and its record during the reign of Senusret III allows the date of his rule to be fixed absolutely between the Dates 1878 – 1841BC.

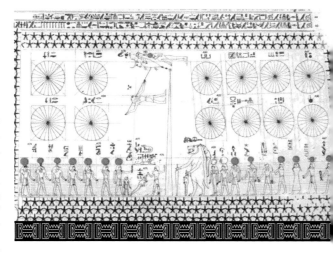

Continued analysis of existing resources and new discoveries means continual refinement of actual dates of events in Ancient Egypt. In this book we've drawn heavily on the work of noted Egyptologist Peter Clayton to provide the best current estimates for the dates of individual pharaoh's reigns.

ABOVE 18th Dynasty astronomical chart recovered from the tomb of Royal Steward Senenmut

Chapter 2

WHERE DID THE ANCIENT EGYPTIANS COME FROM?

RIGHT The
Fertile Crescent

It is clear from the hieroglyphic record and surviving fragments of papyri that the ancient Egyptians were very aware of the history of their kings and the heritage of their civilisation which, according to Manetho, began with the unification of Upper and Lower Egypt. Based on discoveries made at Hierakonpolis, Upper Egypt, in 1897 by the Egyptologist J.E.Quinell that honour belongs to a rather shadowy king, Narmer, around 3150BC. But where did those people that Narmer is credited with unifying over 5,000 years ago come from?

During the 18th and 19th centuries, colonial and imperial historians, guilty of unconscious racism, had difficulty reconciling the evidence of an ancient civilisation with the people of contemporary Egypt. That unconscious racism was based on the spurious science of racial hierarchy based on skin colour, facial features and hair colour, generating the type of charts which appeared in text books as late as the 1950s showing white Caucasians at the top of the table and black aborigines at the bottom.

That kind of antediluvian thinking changed during the latter half of the 20th century, particularly since research by molecular scientists demonstrated that all humans living today, of whatever race, descended from a single small group of people exiting north-east Africa about 150,000 years ago, the so-called "Eve" theory.

But, ignoring the evidence of a mix of racial characteristics in contemporary Egypt, 19th century scientists argued that ancient Egyptians had originally come from Mesopotamia, a region roughly corresponding to modern day Iraq rather than from sub-Saharan or eastern Africa. Modern thinking has rejected this view with the reasonable consensus that Ancient Egyptians were predominantly the indigenous natives of the Nile Valley and north-east Africa though some recent archaeological discoveries have re-opened the Mesopotamian connection.

Historical evidence

To understand the mix of people in ancient Egypt we need to go back to the end of the last ice age, 10,000 years ago, when the Sahara was green and fertile and in the Fertile Crescent Neolithic Stone Age man was deserting a hunter gatherer lifestyle in favour of farming and animal herding. The Fertile Crescent is a semi-circular swathe of land embracing modern day Egypt, Israel, Palestine,

RIGHT Badari figure of a woman carved from hippopotamus ivory c. 4000 BC

OPPOSITE Typical Naqada II pot decorated with ships c. 3500 BC

Lebanon, Iraq, Kuwait, parts of Turkey and Iran and the island of Cyprus.

At that date indigenous tribes with distinct cultures were becoming established in the Nile Valley, Merimde in northern or Lower Egypt and Badari in Upper or southern Egypt but as the climate got hotter and drier there would inevitably have been migration into the Nile Valley: eastwards from the Sahara, which was rapidly becoming a desert, westwards from the Middle East and north from sub-Saharan and eastern Africa. Evidence suggests that migrants from the Middle East, the area referred to as the Levant in antiquity, probably introduced wheat, barley, sheep and goats and, possibly, cattle to the Nile Valley.

Merimde artefacts, particularly pottery, in Lower Egypt share characteristics with both Near Eastern and African cultures, confirming migrations in the Predynastic era. Contemporary, ongoing excavations, particularly in Upper Egypt, have also demonstrated increasing levels of trade between Lower and Upper Egypt in the years 4000 – 5000 BC.

Archaeological evidence

Over time the artefacts of cultures change and develop. Archaeologists

identify the most distinct changes by ascribing new names to fresh cultures, usually the name of places where artefacts demonstrating new and distinct characteristics have been excavated. During the millennium preceding the Predynastic era Lower Egypt's Merimde culture progressed through El-Omari and Maadi cultures while in Upper Egypt the Badari culture was progressively overtaken by three clear stages of the Naqada culture.

These later cultures are distinguished by distinctly foreign objects such as the Gebel el-Arak knife handle with obvious Mesopotamian relief carvings and silver identified as coming from Asia Minor. Egyptian made objects from the period also tend to imitate Mesopotamian styles, items such as cylinder seals and recess panelled architecture.

It is not always clear whether foreign influences arrived by trade, with immigrants or even by invasion. Trade goods from the Near and Middle East are assumed to have arrived by water though whether this was by the Mediterranean or the more circuitous route round Arabia from the Persian Gulf to ports at the northern end of the Red Sea remains a matter of debate. Evidence in Predynastic Naqada tombs confirms the use of

ships around 6,000 years ago while some tantalising rock carvings in the eastern desert hint at ships of Mesopotamian design being dragged from the Red Sea to the Nile.

Molecular evidence

Over the past 30 years advances in molecular biology have revolutionised our understanding both of our origins and the relationship between the different races of the contemporary world. Initial research focused on mitochondrial DNA (mtDNA), non-nuclear DNA only passed down the female line, while later research has been supplemented by analysis of male Y-chromosomes.

Based on geographical markers established by this research various DNA studies have found the gene frequencies of contemporary Egyptians are intermediate between those of the Middle East, the Horn of Africa, Sub-Saharan Africa and Europe though male Y-chromosome (NRY) frequency distributions appear to be more similar to the Middle East than Sub-Saharan Africa or Europe.

In recent years some attempt has been made to analyse the DNA of mummified remains. Many scientists have been dismissive of this research, arguing that DNA does not survive in hot temperatures and that results are often contaminated by modern DNA. The latest techniques however, referred to as next–generation sequencing, where researchers read millions of small fragments of DNA rather than amplifying specific samples, make it much easier to spot contamination.

So far only a few Egyptian mummies have been subjected to DNA analysis and the limited results released so far have generated considerable controversy, both from scientists questioning the analysis techniques and racially motivated groups eager to claim either a black or white heritage for the ancient Egyptians. The DNA of Ramesses III has hinted at Sub-Saharan origins while analysis of the mummies of Tutankhamen and his related family have shown that his parents were brother and sister and that, probably as a result of inbreeding, he was a sickly child.

Current consensus

Once the 19th century racial baggage with its myths of a European origin for the ancient Egyptians has been sloughed off the actual evidence provides a clear and logical conclusion for their origin.

The ancient Egyptians came from, well – they came from Egypt.

At the crossroads of North Africa, East Africa, Sub-Saharan Africa and the Middle East, the indigenous tribes of Egypt would inevitably have experienced some migration from the surrounding areas: typically from Africa into Upper Egypt and from the Middle East into Lower Egypt.

This migration together with levels of pre-historic land and sea trade greater than is often imagined will have seen foreign artefacts, culture and customs borrowed and adapted by the ancient Egyptians.

OPPOSITE Gebel el-Arak knife c.3450 BC

BELOW Egyptian Mummy kept in the Vatican Museum

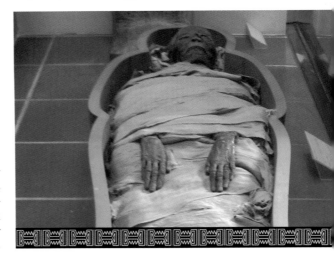

Chapter 3

RELIGION AND THE GOD-KINGS

RIGHT Detail in a frieze from the tomb of Horemheb showing the gods Osiris, Anubis and Horus in order from left to right

The complex system of beliefs, rituals and myths that defined ancient Egypt's religion was an important and integral part of Egyptian society. The features and forms of the religion would prove fluid during the three thousand years or so of Ancient Egypt but the basic tenets of belief were established before the Predynastic era. The Badarian culture's (5500 – 4000BC) cemeteries in Upper Egypt demonstrate the fascination with and veneration of animals that would later play such a prominent role in the visual representation and mythology of the Naqada and Dynastic periods. By contrast, the Merimde culture (4800 – 4300BC) of Lower Egypt had no separate areas for cemeteries and the dead were buried in oval pits within settlements without any grave goods or offerings.

By the Dynastic era religion focused on Egyptians' interaction with myriad deities who were believed to be present in, and in control of, the forces and elements of nature. The myths about this multitude of gods were used to explain the origins and behaviour of the forces they represented and the practices of Egyptian religion were attempts to both provide for the gods and obtain their favour and approval.

These religious practices centred on the pharaoh, the divine king of Egypt. Though human, the pharaoh was believed to have descended from the gods and was expected to act as an intermediary between them and his people, sustaining the gods through rituals and offerings so that they would maintain order in the universe.

Enormous resources were devoted to the performance of these rituals, with the construction of huge temples and other architectural monuments venerating the gods. Another important aspect of Egypt's religion was a belief in the afterlife, characterised by the enormously complex funerary practices surrounding the deaths of pharaohs and their royal family members.

Over time the details of religious belief changed and altered as the importance of particular gods rose and declined with shifts in the intricate relationships between them. At different times some gods became pre-eminent over others, particularly gods such as Ra, the sun god, the creator god Amun and the mother goddess Isis.

These changes were mere detail in a system that endured for several thousand years, surviving foreign rule in the early post Dynastic period until eventually replaced slowly by Christianity in the early centuries AD.

Deities

The phenomena of nature and life were regarded as divine forces in and of themselves by the ancient Egyptians. Their religious customs and practices

were efforts to sustain and placate these phenomena and turn them to human and earthly advantage.

The system of multiple gods, referred to as polytheistic, was very complex, particularly as some deities were believed to have many different manifestations while others had multiple mythological roles. By contrast important natural forces such as the sun were associated with more than one god. The huge sprawl of over 2,000 gods ranged from those with vital roles in the universe to minor deities and demons with very limited functions and power.

Egyptians understood that visual and physical images of the gods were not literal presentations of how they might look and believed the gods' true natures were hidden and mysterious. Instead they existed as symbolic images or stylised icons that defined the god's role in nature. For example, the image of the funerary god Anubis was a jackal, a creature whose scavenging threatened preservation of the body and worked as a way of confronting this threat. The jackal's black skin was symbolic of both mummified flesh and the resurrection implied by the fertile black soil of the Nile Valley.

Many gods were quite parochial, associated just with particular regions and localised cults. Associations with particular regions could change and drift and did not necessarily mean that a god associated with a particular region had originated there. The god Monthu, for instance, was the original patron of the city of Thebes but was ousted from that role and replaced by Amun during the course of the Middle Kingdom. The national popularity and importance of other gods fluctuated in similar ways over time.

Ma'at and mythology

As in most cultures, Egyptian myths were metaphorical stories used to describe and illustrate gods' roles and actions in nature and the role of people in the Egyptians' view of the world and universe. Originally established by oral tradition mythical narratives were rarely written in full with texts usually only containing extracts or episodes from or allusions to a larger well known myth. This means our knowledge of Egyptian mythology derives mainly from hymns that detail specific god's roles, ritual and magical texts which describe actions relating to mythological events and funerary texts which describe the roles of gods in the afterlife.

in terms of the observable cosmos and human society. Egyptians believed Ma'at was under constant threat from forces of disorder and required the forces of all society to maintain stability. On the human level this meant all members of society co-operating and co-existing while at a cosmic level it meant sustaining the gods in balance with the appropriate offerings and rituals.

Tying in with the Egyptian's view of the universe defined by Ma'at and their creation myths was the concept of time. Throughout time's linear passage a cyclical pattern was observed in which Ma'at was renewed by periodic events echoing the original creation. Events such as the annual flooding of the Nile, the succession from one king to another and most importantly, the daily journey across the sky of the sun god Ra.

The creation myths described the earth as a flat expanse of land, personified by the god Geb, overarched by the goddess of the sky Nut, the two regions separated by Shu, the god of air. Beneath the flat earth lay a parallel underworld and undersky and beyond the oversky and undersky lay the infinite expanse of Nu, the chaos that had existed before creation: a surprisingly prescient metaphor for the universe as we understand it today.

Central to Egyptian beliefs were creation myths and a concept of the universe codified in the term Ma'at, a word for both a goddess and the concept of truth, justice and order. Ma'at, in existence since the creation of the world, was the fixed, eternal order of the universe both

LEFT The goddess Ma'at wearing the "Feather of Truth"

ABOVE Ra travelling through the underworld, from the copy of the Book of Gates in the tomb of Ramses I

RIGHT Horus, the falcon-headed god

OPPOSITE BOTTOM "The Judgement", Weighing the Heart from a papyrus of the 19th Dynasty scribe Hunefer

Connected to concepts of an afterlife the Egyptians also believed in a place called Duat, a shadowy and mysterious region associated with death and rebirth. Every day Ra travelled from East to West across the underside of the sky and at night passed through the Duat ready to be reborn at dawn.

The Egyptians pictured their metaphorical universe inhabited by three types of sentient beings: gods, the spirits of dead humans and living humans. Most important among living humans was the pharaoh who was capable of bridging human and divine realms.

One of the most important Egyptian myths was the story of Osiris and Isis which tells of the divine ruler Osiris, murdered by his jealous brother Set. Osiris' sister and wife Isis (an incestuous relationship sometimes replicated in real life Ancient Egypt) resurrected him so that they could conceive an heir, Horus. Osiris then entered the underworld, becoming ruler of the dead, while Horus, as an adult, fought and defeated Set to become king himself.

Set's association with chaos and the restoration of Osiris and Horus as the rightful rulers provides a rational for pharaonic succession and portrays pharaohs as upholders of order and stability. At the same time Osiris' death and rebirth provides a powerful metaphor for the Egyptian agricultural cycle with, each year, crops growing in the wake of the Nile's annual inundation.

Afterlife

Egyptians believed that humans possessed both a ka, a life-force which left the body at the

point of death, and a ba, a set of spiritual characteristics unique to each individual and which, unlike ka, remained attached to the body after death.

Funerary rituals were designed to release the ba from the body so that it could move freely while offerings of food and sustenance were provided to sustain the life of the ka after death so that both ka and ba could re-join and carry on life as an akh.

The ba returned to its body each night to receive new life before emerging every morning as an akh. For that reason Egyptians believed it was important to preserve the dead so that a body remained for the ba to return to each night.

In the early Dynastic period Egyptians believed that only the pharaoh had a ba and only he could become one with the gods while dead commoners passed, instead, into a dark, bleak realm that was the antithesis of life. However by the late Old Kingdom and First Intermediate Period Egyptians began embracing the belief that the possession of ba and the possibility of a paradisiacal afterlife extended to everyone.

By the time of the New Kingdom with its fully developed beliefs in the afterlife the ba or soul had to avoid a series of supernatural tests and dangers in the Duat before undergoing a final judgement known as the "Weighing of the Heart" against "The Feather of Truth". In this judgement the gods compared the actions of the deceased while alive (symbolised by the heart) to Ma'at to determine whether or not he or she had lived a life in accordance with Ma'at. Provided the deceased was considered worthy their ka and ba would be united into an akh.

LEFT Ba represented as a bird with a human head

BELOW Colossal
statue of the 19th
Dynasty Pharaoh
Ramesses II

Divine pharaohs

Though a continuing topic of debate among Egyptologists it seems likely that Egyptians viewed royal authority as itself a divine force and though they recognised the Pharaoh as human and subject to human weaknesses they simultaneously viewed him as a god because the divine power of kingship was incarnated in him.

The pharaoh acted as an intermediary between the people and the gods and was the key to upholding Ma'at, by both maintaining justice and harmony in human society and sustaining approval of the gods with rituals, offerings and temples.

It's likely, too, that a pharaoh's real-life power and influence may have differed from the politically corrected and sanitised version depicted in official writings and depictions and it is clear that towards the end of the New Kingdom their religious influence was declining drastically.

Temples and Tombs

In most religions, belief in ephemeral and transcendental deities has to be sustained with ritual and tangible physical evidence such as iconic statues and temples.

Temples existed from the beginning of Egyptian history, were central to Egyptian society and by the height of the civilisation were present in most of

its towns. These included both mortuary temples to serve the spirits of dead pharaohs and temples dedicated to patron gods although it is sometimes difficult to distinguish between the two because divinity and kingship were so closely entwined.

State run Egyptian temples were built as houses for the gods where physical images and representations of the gods were cared for and provided with offerings. This was to ensure that the gods were sustained and would maintain the equilibrium of the universe. For that reason these temples were seen as vital to the survival of Egyptian society and culture and vast resources were devoted to their upkeep, from both estates owned by the temples and donations from the royal families. Though central to Egyptian society these temples were not intended as places of worship for the general populace and ordinary people had instead their own complex set of religious practices.

From the early days of ancient Egypt and with their belief in an infinite afterlife, pharaohs began building robust stone sarcophagi and tombs to house both them and the goods they would need in that afterlife. Over time these tombs grew larger, more elaborate and

increasingly durable, culminating in massive pyramids designed to advertise the pharaohs' achievements and ensure their immortality. That the tombs have survived and that we still know the names of the pharaohs that built them demonstrates that in one respect they were a complete success. But the speed with which the tombs were ransacked by grave robbers and the gradual erosion of belief in pharaohs' divine status during the New Kingdom raises doubts about ordinary Egyptians unquestioning acceptance of the elaborately structured complex of pharaonic religious beliefs.

ABOVE First pylon and colonnade of the Temple of Isis at Philae

Egypt's most important deities

Over the three thousand years of its civilisation ancient Egypt created a sprawl of over two thousand gods. Many were local and provincial or else minor deities associated with prosaic domestic concerns but here, in alphabetical order, is a useful reference of the most important and enduring gods.

Amun - King of the gods and god of the wind

Anubis - Jackal headed god of the dead and mummification

Anuket - Goddess of the river

Apep - Evil god of chaos and darkness

Aten - Disc of the sun and an aspect of the sun god Ra

Atum - God of creation

Bastet - Goddess of cats, protection, joy, dance, music and love

Bat - Cow goddess, depicted with human face and horns

Bes - Protector of households

Geb - God of the earth

Hapi - God of the annual Nile flooding

Hathor - Goddess of the sky, love, beauty, joy, motherhood, foreign lands, mining, music and fertility

Heb - Deification of infinity, name literally meaning endlessness

Heka - Deification of magic

Hemsut - Goddess of fate and protection

Horus - God of vengeance, sky, protection and war – one of the oldest and most significant Egyptian deities

Isis - Goddess of motherhood, magic and fertility

Khepri - God of rebirth and the sunrise

Khnum - God of creation and the waters

Khonsu - God of youth and the moon

Ma'at - Egyptian concept of truth personified by Ma'at, goddess of truth and justice

Meretseger - Goddess of tomb builders and protector of royal tombs

Meskhenet - Goddess of childbirth
Min - God of fertility

Monthu - God of warfare, sun and valour

Mut - Queen of the goddesses and lady of heaven

Nefertem - God of healing and beauty

Neith - Goddess of war, hunting weaving and wisdom

Nephthys - Goddess of death, service, lamentation and night-time

Nut - Goddess of the sky

Osiris - God of the afterlife

Ptah - God of creation, the arts & fertility

Ra or Re - Ancient Egyptian solar deity, identified with the midday sun

Sekhmet - Goddess of fire, war, vengeance, menstruation and medicine

Seshat - Goddess of writing and wisdom

Set - God of storms, the desert and chaos

Sobek - God of the Nile, the army, military and fertility

Sopdet - Goddess of the star Sirius

Tatenen - God of the primordial mound, identified with creation myths

Taweret - Goddess of fertility and childbirth

Tefnut - Goddess of moisture

Thoth - God of knowledge, hieroglyphs and wisdom

Chapter 4

THE FIRST PHARAOHS

By the fourth millennium BC there were distinct and established cultures in the Nile Valley, the Naqada in Upper Egypt and Merimde in Lower Egypt. These people had become increasingly sedentary and settled as their lifestyle became more reliant on farming and livestock herding with progressively less hunting of wild animals.

According to Manetho the Unification of the Two Lands, Upper and Lower Egypt, under one king was the critical act that defined the start of the ancient Egyptian civilisation. By working back from known astronomical dates and early archaeological data this event has been fixed at around 3100 BC.

The main question is who was this first king who united the two kingdoms? The feat has been ascribed variously to either Narmer or Menes, who may even have been the same person, or possibly king "Scorpion" for whom there is compelling archaeological evidence. Egyptologists now place Scorpion and Narmer sequentially in a Predynastic "Dynasty 0", estimated to have run from 3150 – 3050 BC.

Excavations at Hierakonpolis

Evidence for the early Dynasty 0 kings comes from the discoveries of British Egyptologist James Quibell excavating at Hierakonpolis, Upper Egypt, in 1897-98. Hierakonpolis was the ancient city of Nekhen on the west bank of the Nile north of Aswan and dedicated to the

Dynasty	Period BC	Pharaohs
0	3150 - 3050	"Scorpion"
		Narmer
1	3050 - 2890	Hor-Aha
		Djer
		Djet
		Den
		Aneddjib
		Semerkhet
		Qa'a 2
	2890 - 2686	Hotepsekhemwy
		Raneb
		Nynetjer
		Seth-Peribsen
		Khasekhemy

ABOVE "Scorpion" macehead at the Ashmolean Museum

falcon-headed god Horus. His excavations there produced some remarkable finds such as a gold-headed hawk representing Horus and an almost life-size hollow-cast statue of 6th Dynasty king Pepi I and his son Merenre. The important discoveries relating to the Early Dynastic Period were made in a pit labelled the "Main Deposit" located between the walls of an Old Kingdom and later Middle Kingdom temples. Quibell found objects in this pit that we now know to be the most important physical evidence of the Early Dynastic Period.

These objects consisted of palettes and maceheads including the major piece, the Narmer Palette. The kings Scorpion and Narmer were identified from representations and early hieroglyphics on the pieces. The fragmented Scorpion Macehead portrays a king in full ritual dress with the ritual bull's tail hanging from the back of his belt and wearing the tall White Crown of Upper Egypt. Before the king's face and believed to indicate his name is a scorpion and a seven-petalled flower. The decorative frieze round the remaining top of

the macehead depicts lapwings hanging by their necks from vertical standards. In hieroglyphs lapwings indicate "the common people" and their fate suggests that they have been overcome by a victorious King Scorpion.

Two things can be deduced from this relic: King Scorpion, wearing the White Crown, is only the king of Upper Egypt and there has been a battle in which he has conquered the "lapwings". Wearing just one crown, the White Crown, implies that Scorpion is only the king of Upper Egypt and the event being commemorated pre-dates the unification of Upper and Lower Egypt. By contrast, the Narmer Palette, a monumental piece of dark green slate, portrays Narmer in two aspects, wearing respectively the White Crown of Upper Egypt and the Red Crown of Lower Egypt implying that he is now king of both lands.

Chronologically this suggests that Scorpion precedes Narmer, before unification and that Narmer is the most likely candidate as the king who unified Upper and Lower Egypt.

Later, hieroglyphic convention showed the White and Red Crowns being worn together, one inside the other, forming the *shemty*, the Crown of Upper and Lower Egypt.

The founding of Memphis

By convention Narmer's successor Hor-Aha, who was probably his son, is regarded as the first king of the 1st Dynasty. Hor-Aha's greatest achievement was the founding of the unified country's capital city at Memphis, just south of the apex of the Nile delta. It could be argued that with the potential for flooding this was not a good site but the location was important politically for a newly unified country. Protected by ever strengthened dams the city endured throughout Egypt's history, becoming one of the

greatest cities of the ancient world.

Manetho records that Hor-Aha reigned for an astounding 62 years and only came to an end when he was carried off by a hippopotamus during a hunting expedition when presumably he was already of great age.

First Dynasty tombs

After the founding of Memphis the early Egyptian kings began to construct their tombs at the sacred site of Abydos in middle Egypt while their nobles established their burials on the edge of the desert plateau of Saqqara, overlooking Memphis.

At both sites archaeological evidence is scarce as the struc-

OPPOSITE TOP
Detail of the "Scorpion" macehead showing the scorpion and White Crown of Upper Egypt

OPPOSITE BOTTOM
Both sides of the Narmer Palette at the Egyptian Museum, Cairo

LEFT Copper tool bearing the serekh of Hor-Aha

ABOVE Ruins of the pillared hall of Ramesses II at Memphis

now confirmed as the site of royal burials with Saqqara being the site for prominent nobles. Also at Abydos and dating from the later Predynastic Period there is now recognised a series of tombs that lead into the early royal tombs so that their evolution can be traced through succeeding reigns.

At Saqqara are the remains of a large rectangular tomb, originally incorrectly attributed to Hor-Aha, consisting of 27 storerooms at ground level for funerary equipment and offerings and five rooms below ground. The mudbrick exterior was panelled all round in a style known as "palace façade" which it resembles, a style later copied as a decorative feature on jewellery. On the north side a brick lined pit once held a wooden solar boat. The large tombs of nobles were typical at the Saqqara site and suggest that some nobles were so mighty and influential that they could, in a number of instances, emulate their royal masters with satellite sacrificial burials associated with their tomb.

In 1991 another interesting boat discovery was made at Abydos when a fleet of 12 boats dating from around 3000BC were found buried side by side. At up to 100ft (30m) in length these boats are the oldest surviving large scale vessels in the world.

tures have been badly damaged and heavily looted over the ages. This, combined with lack of decoration on the surviving remains, means it is difficult to attribute ownership of the original tombs. Egyptologists instead have to rely on the evidence of material remains, largely the seals made on clay stoppers of wine and storage jars. These may indicate a royal name or the name of an official responsible for the burial but do not provide reliable provenance of the tomb's original occupant.

Diligent work by Egyptologists over the past century means that Abydos is

Hor-Aha's tomb was eventually correctly identified as B 19 at Abydos, the largest tomb in the north-western section of the cemetery. The tombs of the remaining First Dynasty kings have all now been correctly located at Abydos. The smallest and worst built tomb belongs to Anedjib and may reflect conflict between him and his successor Semerkhet and associated evidence of north versus south dynastic struggle. Re-excavation of the tomb of Qa'a, the last king of the First Dynasty, in 1993 revealed that the tomb had been subject to extensive alterations and enlargements starting with a modest brick-lined burial chamber. At 98½ x 75½ft (30 x 23m) it was small by comparison with other 1st Dynasty tombs and also boasted fewer satellite burials, just 26. This probably reflects the ending of satellite burials during Qa'a's reign, completely in the north and in much reduced numbers in the south at Abydos.

Second Dynasty conflict

Lasting just over 200 years (2890 – 2686BC) there is some doubt about the number of kings in the 2ndDynasty. Manetho makes a claim for nine kings but modern consensus has settled on five

or six. Six if the last king, Khasekhemwy was preceded by Khasekhem or five if Khasekhem merely changed his name to Khasekhemwy after successfully resolving various rebellions in the country.

The 2nd Dynasty was characterised by rumbling disputes between Upper and Lower Egypt. The simmering rivalry between the two regions came to a boiling point during the reign of the fourth king of the Dynasty who came to the throne

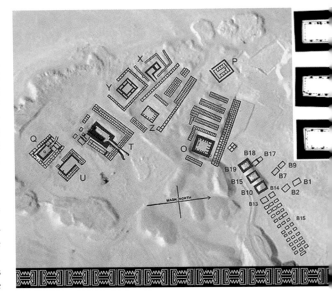

BELOW Hor-Aha's tomb at Abydos, consiting of three chambers (inset) B10, B15 and B19

ABOVE Serekh of Seth-Peribsen on a pottery vase showing the Seth animal instead of the usual Horus raven

RIGHT Seated statue of Khasekhemwy in the Egyptian Museum, Cairo

with the name Sekhemib. The political dispute between north and south had an added religious dimension characterised by the mythological struggle between the two gods Horus and Seth for control of the kingdom of Egypt. Mirroring this proxy dispute, Sekhemib dropped his Horus name in favour of a Seth name, Seth-Peribsen, suggesting that the followers of Seth had gained the upper hand during the ongoing conflicts between the north and south of the country. Seth-Peribsen's granite funerary stele from Abydos provides clear evidence of the change of allegiance. The Horus falcon above the serekh of his Horus name has been replaced by the animal of Seth with its distinctive pointed ears. Seth-Peribsen's successor, Khasekhemwy, appears to have adopted a diplomatic solution by incorporating the names of both gods in the hieroglyph of his own name in an attempt to mollify both religious factions.

But the disputes did continue during Khasekhemwy's reign and prior to his restoration of peace there is evidence that northern aggressors had reached as far south as Nekhen, the ancient capital of the southern kings on the eastern bank of the Nile. The fighting must have been fierce and the contorted bodies round the base of two seated statues of Khasekhemwy suggest that over 47,000 northerners were killed in the final battle. Both statues portray the king wearing the White Crown of Upper Egypt signifying victory over Lower Egyptian enemies but after considerable loss of lives.

ABOVE Shunet el-Zebib, monumental remains at Abydos

Khasekhemy left a huge 230ft (70m) long trapezoidal shaped tomb at Abydos from which, in spite of extensive looting over the years, the kings sceptre of gold and small stone pots decorated in gold leaf have been recovered. About a kilometre away from Khasekhemwy's tomb is the Shunet el-Zebib, one of the world's oldest monumental buildings, dating back almost 5,000 years. Measuring 404 x 210ft (123 x 64m) the building has massive walls 16 ft thick and 66ft high covered with an articulated palace façade. It is unclear whether the building is associated with Khasekhemwy's tomb and what its exact purpose was.

Though looking like a massive fort excavations have revealed evidence of complicated buildings, storerooms perhaps for provisions provided for the king's ka (soul).

The 2nd Dynasty ends with Khasekhemwy but he is also responsible for the start of the next Dynasty. He seemingly married a northern princess, Nemathap, to seal the reconciled relations between the followers of Horus and Seth. Preserved jar seals describe her as "The King-bearing Mother" and she is regarded in later ages as the ancestral figure of the 3rd Dynasty, the first Dynasty of the Old Kingdom.

Chapter 5

THE OLD KINGDOM

The Old Kingdom, lasting over 500 years (2686 – 2181BC) and embracing four Dynasties and 24 known pharaohs, marks Egypt's first long period of stability and also the era when its civilisation became fully established. This was largely due to increasing centralisation of government and the creation of an efficient administrative system.

Kingship also developed and evolved during the Old Kingdom with reinforcement of the concept of the pharaohs' divine status. The kings were now considered to be the incarnation of the god Horus and also, from the 5th Dynasty onwards, son of the sun god Re.

This emphasis on the divine status of the pharaohs is reflected in the monumental nature of their surviving tombs and the Old Kingdom is rightly remembered as the Age of the Pyramid Builders. Still awesome today, the edifices that have survived include Djoser's Step Pyramid at Saqqara, the Great Pyramid of Khufu at Giza and the famous Sphinx, thought to represent the 4th Dynasty king Khafre.

But the security and stability of the Old Kingdom could not last forever and its last Dynasty, the 6th, saw decentralisation of authority with increased autonomy and power being assumed by regional officials. The Old Kingdom ended around 2181BC in a state of political strife and anarchy, heralding in the First Intermediate period and over 100 years of relative chaos and disorder.

Dynasty	Period BC	Pharaohs
3	2686 - 2613	Sanakhte Djoser Sekhemkhet Khaba Huni
4	2613 - 2498	Senfru Khufu (Cheops) Djedefre Khafre (Chepren) Menkaure (Mycerinus) Shepseskat
5	2498 - 2345	Userkaf Sahure Neferirkare Shepseskare Neferefre Niuserre Menkauhor Djedkare Unas
6	2345 - 2181	Teti Pepi I Merenre Pepi II

The Pyramid Builders

Sanakhte, the first pharaoh of the 3rd Dynasty, is little known though his suc- cessor Djoser, believed to be his brother, ensured his immortality by building the Step Pyramid of Saqqara, chronologically the first of the great pyramids.

Both kings were responsible for starting the serious exploitation of the mineral wealth of the Sinai Peninsula, rich in copper and turquoise.

The stability of the 3rd Dynasty should have been assured by Sanakhate's marriage to the female heir of the Second Dynasty's last king, but political tension between the North and South continued during the Dynasty's early years. Djoser, however, was able to establish his rule as far south as Aswan and the First Cataract later became the official southern boundary of Ancient Egypt. Cataracts are the white water rapids that occur on the Nile between Khartoum and Aswan, the First Cataract being the most northerly.

BELOW Djoser's Step Pyramid at Saqqara

The Step Pyramid and mortuary complex at Saqqara

Djoser (2668 – 2649BC) was probably the pharaoh's personal name, appearing only in later records and his Horus name, Netjerikhet, is the name inscribed on all his monuments, including the Step Pyramid complex at Saqqara.

In the Second Dynasty royals were generally buried at Abydos while Saqqara was mainly reserved for officials whose tombs or *mastabas* appeared as a series of low mounds on the skyline looking towards the royal city of Memphis. Djoser however chose Saqqara for his tomb and picked a site about a mile back from the escarpment edge to build his stupendous pyramid and mortuary complex.

As well as being Egypt's first pyramid Djoser's Step Pyramid was also the first structure in the world to be entirely built from stone. Djoser's reign lasted for 19 years, barely enough time perhaps to build the pyramid and extensive mortuary complex but Djoser was able to rely on the incredible skill and resources of his vizier Imhotep, now generally regarded as responsible for the tomb's design and construction.

The concept behind Djoser's monument was to create an area for his spirit focused on the pyramid itself. This began life as a conventional, stone built, *mastaba* which was subsequently enlarged by piling up more *mastabas*, one upon another until it consisted of six unequal steps rising to 204 ft (62m) covering an area 358 x 411ft (109 x 125m). Inside is a honeycomb of shafts and tunnels, including several dug by tomb robbers though it is difficult now to distinguish these from original unfinished tunnels.

Facing the pyramid on the south side of the large enclosure surrounding it is the South Tomb. This includes three carved relief panels showing the king perform-

pyramid lies a wide courtyard with buildings on the east side known as the *heb-seb* court which has been the subject of gradual restoration over the past 40 years.

Djoser's pyramid and funerary complex is an enduring testament to the king's authority. A strong government and effective administration would have been required to organise, house and feed the vast workforce required and Djoser's complex is the first of a long line of stone monuments built with the same reliance on an efficient administration.

LEFT Djoser running for the Hebsed from a relief panel in the South tomb

BELOW Djoser's funerary complex at Saqqara

ing the *heb-seb* ritual which reaffirms his fitness to rule. On one panel he is wearing the tall White Crown and a ritual beard while running a course which underlines the entirely ritualistic nature of the complex created by Imhotep.

Between the South Tomb and the

BELOW Remains of
Meydum Pyramid

OPPOSITE TOP
The "Bent Pyramid",
Snefru's first pyramid
at Dahshur

OPPOSITE BOTTOM
The "Red Pyramid",
Snefru's second
pyramid at Dahshur

Meydum Pyramid

Huni (2637 – 2613BC), the fifth and last king of the third Dynasty, made a radical move in the choice of his burial site, selecting Meydum on the edge of the Faiyum, 50 miles (80km) south of Cairo.

His pyramid was the first with a square ground plan and was intended, also, to be geometrically true. Originally consisting of seven tall steps faced in white Tura limestone and giving it a lighthouse-like appearance, only three steps now remain though these still rise to 214ft (65m).

During the 18th Dynasty, in the New Kingdom, Egyptians relying on contemporary inscriptions believed that the Meydum tomb and pyramid was built by Senfru but evidence now confirms that the pyramid was built for Huni but was completed by his son-in-law and successor Snefru who then went on to build his own two pyramids.

Snefru's two pyramids

Huni was the last of a long line of Memphis kings and his daughter Hetopheres, married Snefru who though also from Memphis was from a different royal family, constituting in Manetho's judgement the start of a new Dynasty, the Fourth Dynasty.

Snefru (2613 – 2589BC) is credited with expeditions beyond the boundaries of Egypt, to the Lebanon to secure cedar for temple doors and great ships and to Sinai for turquoise. Like his predecessor Huni, Snefru also chose to move the royal burial ground, not back to Saqqara but, instead, to a new site at Dahshur, 28 miles (45km) north of Meydum.

Two pyramids were built at Dahshur by Snefru and though Egyptologists long argued about which was built first consensus has now settled on the southern pyramid, known as the Bent, Blunt or Rhomboidal Pyramid because of its unusual shape.

The second, northern, pyramid, known as the Red Pyramid because of the colour of its stone in the setting sun, is significant because it is the first true pyramid though at 43°36' the angle is slighter than the later norm of 51°52'.

Completing his predecessor's pyramid and building two of his own confirms that Snefru had had complete and overwhelming control of the kingdom and its resources. Building on this heritage Snefru's son, Khufu (2589 – 2566BC), was to take his father's achievements even further with the Great Pyramid on the Giza Plain, the very apogee of Egyptian pyramid building.

The Great Pyramid of Giza

According to Manetho the builder of the Great Pyramid was Suphis though he is better known by his Greek name Cheops and its Egyptian form, Khufu. Records suggest that Khufu, like his father, undertook military expeditions to the Sinai Peninsula where rock engravings in the Wadi Maghara confirm the presence of his troops there. A faint inscription on a large boulder on Elephantine Island in

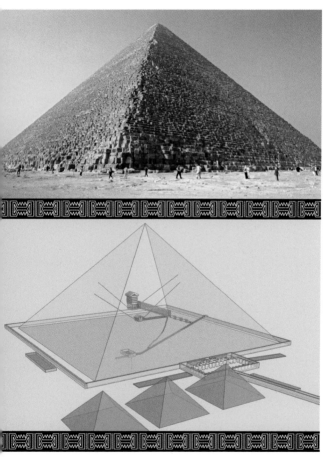

the upper reaches of the Nile suggests that the king had interests in the far south of the country, round Aswan, a source of fine red granite.

Khufu's greatest achievement was the building of The Great Pyramid on the Giza plateau, a monument that was eventually recognised as the first of the Seven Wonders of the Ancient World and the only one still standing. Originally 451ft (127.5m) tall it subsequently lost its top 30ft but remained the world's tallest man made edifice until well into the 19th century, a significant record held for over four and half thousand years.

It is not known why Khufu spurned the royal burial sites at Abydos and Saqqara or the site of his father's pyramid at Dahshur, choosing instead a stretch on the Giza plateau to the south-west of modern day Cairo. During the 23 or 24 years of his reign Khufu channelled all his efforts into this single immense monument rather than several smaller pyramids and tomb complexes. The external structure and dimensions seem to have been set and adhered to from the start though there is evidence that the internal arrangement underwent several changes during construction.

The chief of works for construction of the pyramid is believed to be Hemon,

Khufu's cousin. A robust life size seated statue of Hemon discovered in his *mastaba* close to his masterpiece appears to confirm this view.

The great puzzle of the Great Pyramid, how it was built, has eluded scientists and thinkers over the ages and in spite of practical experiments attempted with either ramps or levers no entirely satisfactory explanation has yet been discovered.

The outside faces of the pyramid were coated in bright white Tura limestone which was almost totally removed during the Middle Ages to build medieval Cairo, along with limestone walls of the massive mortuary temple now represented by just the black basalt floor.

The royal ship of Khufu

An interesting discovery was made in 1954 during clearance work close to the south side of the Great Pyramid when a 101ft long rock-cut pit hermetically sealed with 41 carefully hewn stone blocks was found. Inside the pit were 650 carefully dismantled parts of a 141ft (43m) long ship, too long to fit in the pit without being broken into a kit of parts. Following many years of patient restoration the ship was presented to the world in 1982, housed in a specially designed museum which also incorporates the pit in which the parts had remained undisturbed for 4,500 years.

OPPOSITE TOP
Khufu's Great Pyramid at Giza

OPPOSITE BOTTOM
3D projection of the Great Pyramid's interior

BELOW Khafre's pyramid, the Second Pyramid at Giza

ABOVE Rear view of Sphinx at Giza

The Second Pyramid at Giza

Khufu was succeeded by his son, the short lived Djedefre about whom little is known though, significantly, he was the first king to adopt the name "son of Re", the sun god.

Djedefre opted for a modest burial chamber, unlike either his father or his brother Khafre who succeeded him and erected a pyramid at Giza almost matching his father's in scale and won-der. In fact, though Khafre's pyramid, the Second Pyramid of Giza, is, at 447ft (136.4m) shorter than the Great Pyramid it provides the illusion of being taller because it was built on higher ground, the highest on the Giza plateau. Some of the original Tura limestone casing is still intact at the peak of the Second Pyramid giving an impression, though inadequate, of how the original pyramids would have looked.

Khafre's pyramid complex and its

layout, pyramid, causeway, valley temple and mortuary temple, was to establish the standard for all future Old Kingdom royal tombs. The valley temple is an impressive building and the only stone building apart from the pyramids to have survived from the Old Kingdom. Built from local limestone the temple was then provided with a façade constructed of massive red granite slabs transported north 600 miles from the Aswan quarries.

The Sphinx

An integral part of Khafre's funerary complex at Giza, the Sphinx was apparently carved from an outcrop of local limestone left after the quarrying of blocks for Khufu's Great Pyramid. The crouching human-headed lion represents the god Re-Harakhte, the sun god at his eastern dawn rising, while the face is believed to portray Khafre.

The Sphinx is about 66ft (20m) high and 240ft (73m) long and for most of its 4,500 year existence was covered by windblown sand. Removal of the sand in more recent years has accelerated deterioration of the sphinx until a large piece of rock falling from its right shoulder in 1988 triggered a restoration and conservation programme.

The third pyramid of Giza

Building the pyramids of Khufu and Khafre demanded huge material and people resources and their reigns are believed to have been unrelentingly harsh. By contrast Khafre's son and successor, Menkaure, was more benign and his image in sculptures and portraits seem to possess a degree of benevolence.

His pyramid, the Third Pyramid of Giza, is certainly much smaller than the other two, suggesting, perhaps, more modest aspirations and demands.

Rising to 228ft (70m), the upper half of Menkaure's pyramid was cased in gleaming white Tura limestone while the bottom half was constructed from red Aswan granite which must have provided a striking contrast when the pyramid was first completed.

Three smaller subsidiary pyramids are associated with Menkaure's pyramid and funerary complex the largest of which was the burial chamber for his chief queen Khamerenebty II. She was the eldest daughter of Khafre by his wife Khamerernebty I who, in her turn, was the daughter of Khufu by an unknown queen. Blood ties were clearly strong if not inbred.

there is little evidence of them today other than mounds of rubble.

Though, again, there are few remains today the Fifth Dynasty king Userkaf introduced a new temple feature, the solar temple, which was echoed by his Fifth Dynasty successors.

Userkaf built the first of the eventual five sun-temples or sanctuaries at Abu-Gurob, in the desert south of Saqqara. This established the features adopted by successive kings in a further four solar temples. It consisted of a sturdy podium of mudbrick and limestone topped by a smaller podium and a stumpy obelisk. In front of the obelisk podium was a sun alter which was later to become a feature of Akhenaten's innovative temple devoted to the god Aten in the Eighteenth Dynasty. A causeway led north-west to a valley temple and to the south was a mudbrick representation of the boat of Re.

OPPOSITE Menkaure's pyramid, the Third Pyramid at Giza

LEFT Statue of Menkaure wearing the White Crown and flanked by representations of the godesses Hathor and Bat

BELOW Typical presentation of a Fifth Dynasty solar temple

The solar temple of Abu-Gurob

The memorial tombs of the Fourth Dynasty kings represented the zenith of pyramid building and though Old Kingdom kings of the Fifth and Sixth Dynasties continued to build pyramids they were modest by comparison and

Chapter 6

THE FIRST
INTERMEDIATE PERIOD

Both historical evidence and Manetho confirm the that Sixth Dynasty and the Old Kingdom came to an end with the death of Pepi II, the last king of the Dynasty, though the events predicating the Dynasty's demise were signposted long before his death. Pepi II's death merely crystallised events that then led to over 100 years of disorder with fragmentation of authority and different regional forces battling for overall power. This long lasting era of relative chaos is described by historians as the First Intermediate Period while they refer to the following period, with stability once again restored, as the Middle Kingdom.

As with most political change no single event accounted for the end of the Sixth

Dynasty	Period BC	Pharaohs
7 & 8	2181 - 2161	Wadjkare
		Qakare Iby
9 & 10	2160 - 2040	Meryibre Khety
		Merykare
		Kaneferre
		Nebkaure
		Akhoty
11	2134 - 2060	Intef I
		Intef II
		Intef III

was marked by confusion and conflict. And the third trigger was a period of drought accompanied by several years of low Nile inundations and low crop yield eventually leading to famine across Ancient Egypt.

OPPOSITE Nileometer on Elephantine Island, Aswam. A series of steps used to measure and record the extent of the Niles annual innundation

70 rulers in 70 days

Humour in 300BC was not that different from today and we can understand completely that Manetho's description of the 7th Dynasty as "70 kings in 70 days" was amusing hyperbole explaining a period of extreme chaos.

Papyri from the later Middle Kingdom confirm that following Pepi II's death central government broke down and the unity of north and south that had been carefully sustained during the Old Kingdom finally fractured, leaving the country in a state of political and monarchical disorder.

The 7th Dynasty was quickly followed by the 8th Dynasty which according to Manetho had as many as 17 kings during its short 20 year life. These kings, possibly descended from Pepi II, claimed to

Dynasty but historians today have identified three main factors accounting for the change. Firstly, and perhaps most importantly, the decentralisation of control away from the royal city of Memphis as provincial governors (nomarchs) acquired regional power and autonomy paying little more than lip service to Memphis by the end of the Old Kingdom. Buying their loyalty coupled with the heavy demands of Egypt's foreign interests rapidly depleted the pharaohs' treasury. Secondly, the extremely long reign of Pepi II: he is estimated to have been in his 90s when he died and as by then he had been pre-deceased by most of his expected successors the transition

rule the country from Memphis though it's likely their authority was limited to the city as the Delta had been invaded by so-called "Asiatics" from the east and the rest of the country was largely controlled by regional *nomarchs*.

There is more tangible evidence of the 8th Dynasty than the 7th but nothing to support Manetho's claim of 17 kings. The little we have is an exemption decree issue by King Wadjkare (Horus name Demedjibtawy) and a small pyramid of a king called Qakare Iby.

Herakleopolitan Kings

Following the death of Pepi II and the breakdown of the Memphite government the provinces made a grab for power with many nomarchs setting themselves up as petty warlords.

From this jostling for power one family from Herakleopolis attained prominence and was able to establish the 9th Dynasty, possibly under King Meryibre Kety. Scant evidence suggests they may have recovered control over the whole country but within 30 years and the start of the second Herakleopolitan dynasty (the 10th Dynasty) there was a reversion to dual sovereignty with southern Egypt now controlled by a rival family, the 11th Dynasty, based at Thebes.

The two Herakleopolitan dynasties (9th and 10th) were relatively unstable with frequent changes of ruler up to the point the 11th Dynasty king Mentuhotep I (2060 – 2010BC) reunited the country.

The rise of the Theban Kings

Evidence supports the view that there was an invasion of Upper Egypt at about the same time as the founding Herakleopolitan 9th Dynasty. This invasion by Intef, the nomarch of Thebes, established a line of Theban kings identified as belonging to the 11th and 12th Dynasties. Intef, referred to as "keeper of the door of the South" is credited with organising an independent ruling body of Upper Egypt though without claiming the title of king. The title, however, was claimed by his successors, also named Intef, and from the southern Theban stronghold Intef II began an assault on the north which was completed and consolidated by Intef III by capturing Abydos and gaining control of Middle Egypt against the Herakleopolitan kings of Lower Egypt.

The first three kings of the 11th Dynasty (Intef I, II and III) were also the last kings of the historical First Intermediate Period and were succeeded by a line of 11th Dynasty kings all, in what starts to look like a tradition, bearing the same name, Mentuhotep.

Mentuhotep II was the king who eventually, around 2033BC, defeated the Herakleopolitan kings, unified Upper and Lower Egypt and heralded in the Middle Kingdom, another long stable period when Ancient Egypt was governed as a single country through the long lasting 11th and 12th Dynasties.

Art and Architecture

The 130 years or so of the First Intermediate Period with the country split and ruled by different sets of rulers is marked by a divergence of art and building styles.

In the north the Memphite kings retained the Memphite artistic tradition and though the art and tombs do not begin to compare to the quality and size of those of the Old Kingdom there are still the familiar reliefs of servants making provision for the dead as well as traditional offering scenes which mirror those of the Old Kingdom Memphite tombs.

ABOVE Drawing of an ebony wand bearing the royal titulary of Meribre Khety, believed to be the first pharaoh of the 9th Dynasty

ABOVE Lively 11th Dynasty Theban style of painting in the tomb of nomarch Khety

OPPOSITE Funerary stele of Intef II carved from limestone

Wooden coffins continued to be used but during the reign of the Herakleopolitan kings these were more elaborately decorated with spells and maps for use in the afterlife painted on the inside.

The rise of the Theban kings introduced a new provincial style of art and architecture generally regarded as more crude and austere than in the old Kingdom because they initially lacked a long tradition of skilled artists and artisans. The artworks of traditional scenes that have survived, though, possess vigour with the use of bright colours and the distorted proportions of human figures. This distinctive style is typified by the rectangular stone slabs (stelae) in the

Theban tombs at Naqa el-Deir.

The funerary complexes of the 11th Dynasty Theban kings centred round rock cut tombs known as saff tombs such as those at El-Tarif. This new style of mortuary architecture included a large courtyard with colonnades carved out of rock at the back wall. Individual burial chambers were cut into the walls facing the central courtyard, allowing for several people to be buried in a single tomb complex. The generally unpainted burial chambers have an austere look which may have been a deliberate choice but more likely implies there was a shortage of skilled artists.

Chapter 7

THE MIDDLE KINGDOM

Historians mark the start of the Middle Kingdom half-way through the 11th Dynasty when Mentuhotep I was successful in reuniting Upper and Lower Egypt. But at the heart of the Middle Kingdom is the 12th Dynasty, a remarkably stable period of 200 years overseen by just eight pharaohs, including 45 year reigns by both Senusret I and Amenenhet III, the last great ruler of the Dynasty.

Important aspects of this era were the recovery of centralised government and the diminishment of local nomarch's authority, introducing the concept of a co-regent to share the responsibility of kingship and a strengthening of military force. Military force, used to defend the country and protect trade routes, was a

Dynasty	Period BC	Pharaohs
11	2060 - 1991	Mentuhotep I
		Mentuhotep II
		Mentuhotep III
12	1991 - 1782	Amenenhet I
		Senusret I
		Amenenhet II
		Senusret II
		Senusret III
		Amenenhet III
		Amenenhet IV
		Queen
		Sobeknefru

the 12th Dynasty and, at the same time, the Middle Kingdom came to a remarkably sudden end with the last pharaoh, Queen Sobeknefru, a co-regent assuming the role after, presumably, the premature death of her predecessor, Amenemhet IV.

11th Dynasty reunification

The First Intermediate period ended with the 10th Dynasty Herakleopolitan kings locked in conflict with the 11th Dynasty Theban kings for overall control of Egypt.

OPPOSITE Painted seated statue of Mentuhotep I

BELOW Wooden model of Egyptian spearmen found in the tomb of Mesehti, an 11th Dynasty nomarch

persistent feature of the Dynasty though the reign of Senusret was notably peaceful with his emphasis on civic works and improved domestic relations with provincial elites.

Much of the vigour of the 12th Dynasty may be related to a change of Pharaonic blood line when Amenemhet, the vizier of Mentuhotep and a man of humble origins, became king around 1991BC. The presumption is that Amenemhet, with the backing of his 10,000 men overthrew and possibly murdered Mentuhotep III, cutting short his brief six year reign.

After almost 200 years of settled rule

ABOVE Mentuhotep I receiving an offering

OPPOSITE TOP Mentuhotep I's temple tomb at Deir el-Bahari

OPPOSITE BOTTOM Map showing Wadi Hammamat, an important site of stone quarries for sourcing tomb and temple building materials

inscriptions confirm him as "Uniter of the Two Lands" and his success is also attested by the series of Horus names he adopted: first, "He who gives heart to the two lands", then "Lord of the White Crown" (Upper Egypt and finally, as we've seen, "Uniter of the Two Lands". There is something suitably symbolic about his victory: Mentuhotep means literally "Montu is content" and Montu was the Theban god of war.

Mentuhotep I ruled for over 50 years and the latter part of his reign saw a return of peace and prosperity to Egypt, evidenced by significant building works at a number of sites such as el-Kab, Gebelein, Deirel-Ballas, Dendara and Abydos. Mentuhotep's greatest building project was his temple tomb on the west bank at Thebes, nestled in the great sway of cliffs at Deir el-Bahari, south of his Theban predecessors saff tombs.

After years of bitter fighting, victory and resolution of the problem fell to Mentuhotep I, the fourth king of the 11th Dynasty, in about 2033BC. The turning point in this grumbling war of attrition happened when the Thinite (Abydos) *nome* rose up in revolt. Mentuhotep took immediate action to crush the revolt and in a series of ensuing battles was able to gain control over the whole country and again unite Upper and Lower Egypt. By the end of his reign

Already old when his father died, Mentuhotep II used his brief 12 year reign to build on his predecessor's achievements by maintaining a defensive stance towards neighbours on northern frontiers and continuing to develop trade links south of the First Cataract. Mentuhotep continued to invest resources in building works and mounted expeditions to source building materials, such as the expedition to Wadi Hammamat to secure stone suitable for temple statues.

Usurping power

The Saqqara and Abydos king lists suggest that Mentuhotep II was the last king of the 11th Dynasty while from the remaining fragments of the Royal Canon of Turin it appears there were seven years without a king between Mentuhotep II's reign and Amenemhet I, the first king of the 12th Dynasty.

There is, however, sketchy evidence of a short six year reign by Nebtawyre Mentuhotep III that fills this gap. His name, together with that of his vizier Amenemhet occurs on a slate bowl found at el-Lisht and dated to Amenemhet I's reign as the first king of the 12th Dynasty.

Historians may be guilty of jumping to the wrong conclusion but the evidence that Amenemhet the vizier and Amenemhet I are the same person is quite compelling. The vizier Amenemhet is well known from a long inscription he left in the Wadi Hammamat. This records that he went to the Wadi with an army of 10,000 men to seek and retrieve a fine block of stone suitable for the lid of the king's (Mentuhotep III)

BELOW Head of
Amenemhet I on a
carved and painted
lintel found in his
mortuary temple
found at el-Lisht

sarcophagus. The inscription records that the stone was successfully sourced and detached but to date no tomb or stone sarcophagus of Mentuhotep III has ever been found.

The general conclusion is that the stone was never used by the king as Amenemhet, supported by his army of 10,000 men overthrew his master, proclaimed himself king and thereby established a new Dynasty, the 12th.

The strength of the 12th Dynasty

Amenemhet I appears to have come from quite humble parents. An inscription from Karnak records a "god's father" Senusret, a commoner in other words, while his mother, Nefert, came from the area of Elephantine. This confirms his Upper Egyptian origin with a religious allegiance to the god Amun and it is from this period in Egypt that Amun comes to prominence, taking over from Montu, god of war and the supreme Theban deity.

Following his enthronement in 1991BC Amenemhet's first act was a comprehensive military patrol of Egypt, cruising the Nile with his fleet and crushing any remaining awkward nomarchs. Having cowed internal opposition he then turned his attention to defeat of Asiatic and Nubian enemies on Egypt's eastern and southern borders.

He then established a new city, remote from Thebes and Herakleopolis but about 20 miles south of Memphis, conveniently placed to control both Upper and Lower Egypt. Amenemhet called his new city Itj-tawy which translates literally as "Seizer of the Two Lands".

Twenty years into his thirty year long reign Amenemhet chose to do something which was to set a precedent for future pharaohs but which also proved particularly fortuitous when Amenemhet's rule came to its sudden end. He associated his son Senusret I with his reign by appointing him as co-regent. For the next 10 years they shared the throne and Senusret

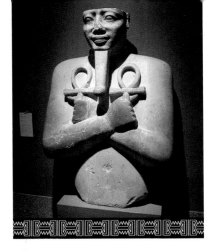

I maintained the military profile with frequent expeditions required to defend and control the country's borders. It was on one such of these expeditions, when Amenemhet had despatched Senusret I to chastise the Libyans of the western desert that disaster struck.

Murder in the bedchamber

Taking advantage of Senusret's absence, conspirators at Amenemhet's court crept into the royal bedchamber at dead of night and set upon the king as he lay asleep, stabbing him to death. Fortunately loyalists were able very quickly to get a message to Senusret who returned sooner than expected and was able to quash the

rebellion before it could spread and then immediately establish himself as the new sole king. The old king's decision to create a co-regent had been astute and as well as maintaining the royal line Senusret went on to have a very successful 34 year long reign and, in a repeat of history, also make his son Amenemhet II co-regent some years before his own death.

Senusret completed the arrangements for the burial of his father in the tomb Amenemhet I had prepared at el-Lisht. Amenemhet I had returned to the pyramidal designs of the 5th and 6th Dynasties, as a way, some commentators have suggested, of legitimising his regime and disguising the way he had seized power at the end of the 11th Dynasty.

LEFT Osiride pillar statue of Senusret

BELOW Amenhemet's eroded pyramid at el-Lisht

BELOW Bust of
Amenhemet II at
Egyptian Museum
of Berlin

RIGHT 12th Dynasty
jewellery demonstrating
a high level of artistic
skill

OPPOSITE TOP
Modern day view
of the Faiyum Oasis

Foreign policy initiatives

Senusret I was succeeded after his death by his son Amenemhet II in 1926BC and continued the family tradition of long reigns with one that lasted 34 years. Amenemhet II worked mainly at consolidating the military and diplomatic work of his predecessors but there is ample evidence that he cultivated diplomatic and trade relations with Egypt's foreign neighbours.

This evidence includes records of expeditions to the Red Sea and what the Egyptians called the Land of Punt (modern day Horn of Africa and southern Arabia) along with evidence of diplomatic gifts exchanged between Egypt and the Levant. These include Egyptian jewellery bearing Senusret I's cartouche in the royal tombs at Byblos in Lebanon together with faithful copies of typical 12th Dynasty jewellery.

South of Luxor archaeologists have uncovered treasure consisting of four large bronze boxes with Amenemhet II's name inscribed on the lids. The boxes contained a large number of silver cups of Levantine and Aegean origin, Babylonian cylinder seals and lapis lazuli amulets from Mesopotamia. At the time silver was more precious than gold in Egypt and the hoard is believed to be a diplomatic gift or tribute to Amenemhet II.

Peace and stability

In what starts to look like a family tradition of alternating names Senusret II succeeded his father Amenemhet around 1895BC having being associated with his father as co-regent for at least three years prior to that. Compared to his militaristic predecessors his almost 20 year reign was a peaceful one.

Inscriptions on the great tombs of nomarch's at Ben Hassan in Middle Egypt confirm that Senusret II had established very good relationships with provincial elites but his main achievement was expansion of cultivation in the Faiyum oasis region west of Giza. Here he began work on an extensive irrigation system of dykes and canals designed to radically increase the amount of cultivable land in that region. The importance of this project is emphasised by Senusret II's decision to move the royal burial ground from Dahshur to El-Lahun, where he built his pyramid.

Close to this pyramid the Egyptologist Flinders Petrie discovered the "pyramid town" built for the workers employed on its construction. Now known as Kahun, the town's original name was Hetep-Senusret which translates as "Senusret is satisfied". Like Pompeii the

town seems to have been suddenly abandoned, leaving behind many possessions which provide a fascinating insight into the social and economic life of the ancient Egyptians. Prosperity and status in the community were revealed by the different sizes and quality of the houses

BELOW Pectoral of Senusret II found in the tomb of Sithathoriunet, believed to be his daughter, at el-Lahun (Kahun)

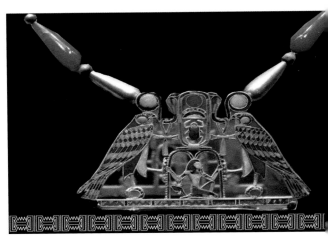

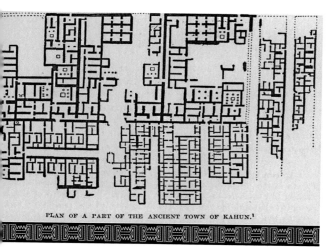

PLAN OF A PART OF THE ANCIENT TOWN OF KAHUN.¹

ABOVE Plan of part of "pyramid town" produced by Professor Flinders Petrie

while dozens of papyri covering topics from accounts and legal documents to gynaecological and veterinary texts have added greatly to our knowledge of the administration and logistics of a multi-racial and highly disciplined workforce.

The high point of the Dynasty

Senusret II's son Senusret III provided a complete contrast to the peaceable and almost benign attitudes of Senusret II. With Senusret III's long reign, 37 years, and that of his son Amenemhet III, 45 years, we

reach the highpoint of the 12th Dynasty.

Senusret III demonstrated great administrative competence as well as being an outstanding military leader. Manetho describes Senusret as a great warrior and comments on his enormous height – "4 cubits, 3 palms and 2 fingers" – about 6ft 6" (2m). This towering presence must have been helpful in cowing the regional nomarchs which he did by creating a new system of government that curtailed their autonomy. It involved dividing the country into three administrative departments, the North, the South and the Head of the South (Elephantine and Lower Nubia), with each one administered by a council of senior staff reporting to a vizier reporting directly to Senusret III.

Once the country's internal governance had been resolved, Senusret III turned his attentions to foreign affairs and soon demonstrated his military competence with a series of devastating campaigns in Nubia. These were aimed at securing Egypt's southern borders against its aggressive neighbours and also safeguarding access to trade routes and the mineral resources, particularly gold, of Nubia.

A series of forts were built along the Nile beyond Aswan, by both Senusret III and his predecessors, and to improve

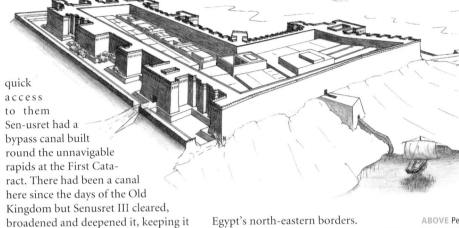

quick
access
to them
Sen-usret had a
bypass canal built
round the unnavigable
rapids at the First Cata-
ract. There had been a canal
here since the days of the Old
Kingdom but Senusret III cleared,
broadened and deepened it, keeping it
maintained throughout his reign.

Inscriptions record that Senusret III successfully and ruthlessly quelled Egypt's Nubian neighbours on a number of occasions. He was apparently proud of his military ability in subduing the Nubians and an impressive stele at Semna (now in the Berlin Museum) records that "I carried off their women, I carried off their subjects, went forth to their wells, smote their bulls: I reaped their grain and set fire thereto".

Most of Senusret III's military campaigns were directed against Nubia but there is record of one campaign in Syria, seemingly a raid of retribution and plunder rather than any desire to extend Egypt's north-eastern borders.

At 350ft (107m) square Senusret III's pyramid at Dahshur was the largest of the 12th Dynasty but scavenging of its limestone casing has, by today, caused severe erosion of its mudbrick core.

Building on the internal, foreign and trade security established by Senusret III his son and successor Amenemhet III used his own long reign to promote economic growth and add to the country's resources. As well as continuing to develop the agricultural potential of the Faiyum, Amenemhet III was singularly successful in exploiting the stone quarries of Egypt and the turquois mines in Sinai. In spite of his long reign there are surprisingly few inscriptions

ABOVE Perspective reconstruction of the Nile fort at West Semna, Nubia

to Amenemhet III in Egypt but over 50 rock inscriptions in Sinai recording almost continuous mining expeditions from the second year of his reign up to his death.

Ending with a whimper

From the commanding heights achieved by Senusret III and Amenemhet III the

12th Dynasty just seems to have fizzled out in its final years. Numerous inscriptions the length of Egypt, from Syria down to the Third Cataract, confirm that Amenemhet III was the last great ruler of the 12th Dynasty as virtually nothing is known about his two successors, Amenemhet IV and Queen Sobeknefru.

It may be that Amenemhet IV, who perhaps died prematurely, never ruled

independently, but ruled first as a co-regent with his father and then, following Amenemhet III's death, with Queen Sobeknefru. There is some evidence that suggests she ruled in her own right for a short time.

Though the transition from the 12th to the 13th Dynasty appears to have happened without any great drama it does mark the end of the Middle Kingdom and the start of another period of relative chaos in ancient Egypt's history described as the Second Intermediate Period.

LEFT Seated statue of Amenemhet III at the Egyptian Collection of the Hermitage Museum, Moscow

BELOW Drawing by Flinders Petrie of cylinder seal of Queen Sobeknefru

Chapter 8

THE SECOND INTERMEDIATE PERIOD

Egyptologists conventionally saw the Second Intermediate Period as another two hundred year era of comparative disorder separating the administrative stability and military strength of the Old Kingdom's 12th Dynasty and the established five hundred year rule by the powerful kings of the New Kingdom. (1570 – 1070BC)

Today historians recognise that for 70 years the 13th Dynasty sustained the control and stability of the 12th Dynasty but the following 100 years or so are characterised by fragmentation of countrywide rule as local kings vied for control of their regions and Semitic ("Asiatic") invaders established power and control in the north-eastern Delta region.

One of the problems historians have in interpreting the Second Intermediate period is the paucity of evidence, either lost in regions frequently inundated by floods or else deliberately destroyed by immediate successors eager to remove all traces of aberrant Dynasties.

The 13th Dynasty

The 12th Dynasty ended with the death of Queen Sobeknefru after a short four year reign and although she left no heirs the transition to the 13th Dynasty seems to have been quite smooth. Records indicate that 10 kings ruled during the 70 years of the 13th Dynasty, ruling from the city Itj-tawy established by Amenemhet I near the Faiyum and continuing to control both Lower and Upper Egypt.

Dynasty	Period BC	Pharaohs
13	1782 - 1720?	Wegaf
		Ameny Intef IV
		Hor
		Sobekhotep II
		Khendjer
		Sobekhotep III
		Neferhotep I
		Sobekhotep IV
		Ay
		Neferhotep II
14	1740? - 1660?	Nehesy
		Merdjefare
		Sewadjkare III
15	1663 - 1555	Sheshi
		Yakubher
		Khyan
		Apepi I
		Apepi II
16	1663 - 1555	Anathar
		Yakobaam
		(Thebes)
17	1663 - 1570	Sobekemsaf II
		Intef VII
		Tao I
		Tao II
		Kamose

ABOVE Life-size wooden statue of King Hor Auyibre's Ka

Few monuments or architectural remains have survived from the 13th Dynasty and our knowledge of the kings is scant, relying on fragmentary inscriptions and the burial site of Hor, the Dynasty's third king, whose nearly intact tomb was discovered at Dahshur in 1894. Historians have suggested that this site was chosen to indicate continuity with

RIGHT Marked in orange is the area believed to have been controlled by the 14th Dynasty

the very successful 12th Dynasty.

Though pillaged in antiquity, the tomb still housed a *naos* containing a rare life-size wooden statue of the dead king's *ka*. Now in Cairo's Egyptian Museum this statue is frequently reproduced as one of the best preserved and artistically most accomplished wooden statues to have survived from ancient Egypt.

Though the reasons are still obscure the demise of the 13th Dynasty seems to be associated with the increasing influence of the separate 14th Dynasty, running apparently concurrently with the 13th Dynasty, and the invasion or mass migration into the north-eastern Delta region of the so-called Hyksos people.

The 14th Dynasty and the rise of the Hyksos kings

Our knowledge of the 14th Dynasty is very scarce with uncertainty about its length, 75 or 150 years, and even when it started. Ruling from the city of Avaris and apparently only controlling the region of the Nile Delta, some scholars have argued that it started before the end of the 12th Dynasty and then ran contemporaneously with the 13th Dynasty. Contemporary consensus believes

the 14th Dynasty, founded by provincial rulers of Canaanite descent, started at some time during the 13th Dynasty and probably lasted into the same era as the 15th Dynasty.

Though the 13th Dynasty had lost control of the Delta region, evidence of trade between the regions controlled by the 13th and 14th Dynasties suggests that relations between the two were not, at least, unfriendly.

Manetho's records indicate as many as 76 14th Dynasty kings while the fragments of the Royal Canon of Turin show there

LEFT Depiction of "Asiatic" people, Hyksos perhaps, migrating into Egypt around 1900BC

would not be enough space on the papyrus for more than 50 kings. Though more evidence is slowly being uncovered there is only currently strong evidence for one 14th Dynasty king, Nehesy, with partial and fragmentary evidence pointing to two other pharaohs, Merdjefare and Sewadjkare III, at uncertain dates around 1700BC.

Further clouding the interpretation of the Delta based 14th Dynasty is the gradual movement into the region of the Hyksos and the eventual establishment of the 15th Dynasty by Hyksos kings. The name Hyksos derives from an Egyptian expression meaning "rulers of foreign lands" which embraces all foreign lands but is used in a contemporary context to describe the infiltration into the Nile Delta of people from Egypt's north-eastern borders, Semites, Canaanites and Phoenicians from the Levant and Western Asia. Debate has explored the idea of the Hyksos arriving suddenly as an invading horde or, as is more likely, by a sort of creeping migration of nomadic and seminomadic tribes including, possibly, foreign warlords seeking employment as mercenaries by Egyptian rulers.

One compelling theory sees foreigners of the 14th Dynasty arriving peaceably to trade while the 15th Dynasty arrived as warlike conquerors who at some stage sacked the city of Memphis though preferred to retain the Delta city of Avaris as their stronghold. The reason it is hard to ratify the swirl of existing theories is the paucity of evidence, destroyed by a continuous sequence of flooding but, more particularly, by the deliberate destruction of all evidence of foreign invasion by later controlling Dynasties eager to remove all trace of occupation by foreign rulers.

Lion inscribed with the cartouche of Khyan, at the British Museum

From the sparse remains and existing resources it has been possible to identify five 15th Dynasty Hyksos kings and also establish links with Crete for the third ruler Khyan. Running contemporaneously with the 15th Dynasty in the Delta region was the shadowy 16th Dynasty. This was almost certainly made up of minor kings or warlords ruling solely by the authority of the 15th Dynasty kings. So far only two 16th Dynasty names, Anathar and Yakobaam, have been identified from scarabs found in northern Egypt and southern Palestine.

The rise of the 17th Dynasty

With the end of the 13th Dynasty and the Hyksos kings of the 15th and 16th Dynasties controlling the north of the country a new line of Egyptian rulers, the 17th Dynasty, was evolving in Thebes. These Theban kings controlled an area from Elephantine in the south to Abydos in the north and were successful in sustaining the culture of the Middle Kingdom.

The first rulers of the 17th Dynasty lived in an uneasy harmony with the Hyksos kings but later kings were more militant and rose against the Hyksos in a series of battles that finally culminated in the foreigners been driven from Egypt.

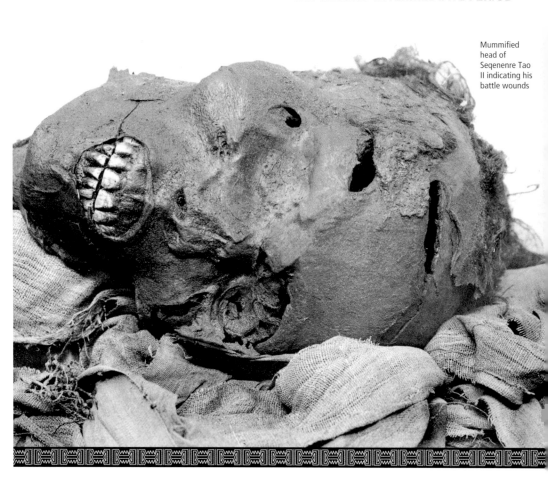

Mummified head of Seqenenre Tao II indicating his battle wounds

The fourth king, Seqenenre Tao II was probably killed on one of these battles since his mummy, discovered in the royal cache at Deir el-Bahari in 1881, shows evidence of mortal head wounds.

Defeating the Hyksos

Ultimately his death was not in vain as the battle against the Hyksos was continued by his sons Kamose and Ahmose I. Kamose's battles and his eagerness to rid Egypt of the Hyksos are well recorded on two steles from Karnak and a writing board known as the Carnarvon Tablet now in the British Museum. Kamose's reign was short, just three years, and his successor, his brother Ahmose I, seems to have maintained a fragile peace with the Hyksos during the early part of his rule.

But about half-way through his 24 year reign Ahmose I mounted a series of attacks against Memphis, Avaris and other Hyksos strongholds. After several hard-fought battles the Hyksos were finally defeated and driven out of Egypt into Palestine.

The successful expulsion of the Hyksos from Egypt marked the start of the 18th Dynasty, with Ahmose I as its first king, and the inauguration of the New Kingdom.

THE NEW KINGDOM

With its establishment as a ruling empire there is little doubt that the 500 year long New Kingdom marks a high point in ancient Egypt's civilisation, its three long lasting Dynasties, the 18th , 19th and 20th, in stark contrast to the five confused and overlapping dynasties of the preceding, shorter and unstable Second Intermediate Period.

Underlining their status as god-like beings the New Kingdom pharaohs left immense works, temples tombs and fortresses which echo the monumental splendour of the 4th and 5th Dynasty pyramids and, closer to our current era, the volume, quality and preservation of surviving artefacts has illuminated in much greater detail our knowledge of the New Kingdom in contrast to our

Dynasty	Period BC	Pharaohs
18	1570 - 1293	Ahmose I
		Amenhotep I
		Tuthmosis I
		Tuthmosis II
		Tuthmosis III
		Queen Hatshepsut
		Amenhotep II
		Tuthmosis IV
		Amenhotep III
		Amenhotep IV
		Smenkhkare
		Tutankhamun
		Ay
		Horemheb
19	1293 - 1185	Ramesses I
		Seti I
		Ramesses II
		Merneptah
		Amenmesses
		Seti II
		Siptah
		Queen Twosret
20	1185 - 1070	Setnakhte
		Ramesses III
		Ramesses IV
		Ramesses V
		Ramesses VI
		Ramesses VII
		Ramesses VIII
		Ramesses IX
		Ramesses X
		Ramesses XI

knowledge of preceding Dynasties.

This is, in part, the consequence of an historical quirk when, conscious of the depredations of tomb robbers, many of the Dynasty's mummies were removed for safety to two great hidden caches, one at Deir el-Bahari and one in the Valley of the Kings. Discovered in the 19th century we now have the opportunity to look directly at these historic faces of the New Kingdom pharaohs and undertake detailed analysis of their remains.

Five hundred years is a long historical period and it would be wrong to view the New Kingdom as a half millennium of unbroken stability. It had its dramatic moments. These include Queen Hatshepsut usurping power, Tuthmosis III strengthening the Empire, Ramesses III repulsing the Sea Peoples and Akhenaten's unsuccessful attempt to establish a monotheistic

OPPOSITE Tuthmosis raising two obelisks, depicted in the Palace of Ma'at, Karnak

ABOVE Panorama of the Valley of the Kings, looking north

religion followed by a drastic change in the royal line triggered by the premature death of the frail boy-king Tutankhamun.

Though 20th Dynasty king Ramesses III successfully defeated the Sea Peoples the heavy cost of this war slowly depleted Egypt's treasury and contributed to the decline of the Egyptian Empire. This decline was exacerbated by internal problems such as food rationing and the first recorded strike by labourers.

Ramesses III was followed by a series of kings all named Ramesses each of whom were increasingly beset by drought, famine, civic unrest and official corruption.

The power of the Dynasty's last Pharaoh, Ramesses XI, was so weakened that in the south the Theban Priests of Amun had assumed power in Upper Egypt while Smendes, founder of the 21st Dynasty, had seized control of Lower Egypt even before the death of Ramesses XI.

Securing the Empire

The first two kings of the 18th Dynasty, Ahmose I and Amenhotep each had long quarter of a century reigns and devoted those reigns to securing Egypt's borders following the expulsion of the Hyksos and re-establishing the country's internal administration.

This was largely accomplished in Ahmose I's reign with a series of campaigns to seal the Syrian border in the north and keep Nubia in order in the south. Ahmose improved control and administration of Upper and Lower Egypt by devolving responsibility to local government in the nomes and ensuring their loyalty to his regime with gifts of land.

Amenhotep I was also responsible for military campaigns, both in Nubia and Libya, but his principal legacy was the start of the Karnak temple complex.

Unusually Amenhotep I was not succeeded by an heir on his death but instead by a military man, Tuthmosis I. Tuthmosis I was already middle aged when he assumed power and it is reasonable to assume he acted as a co-regent during the final years of the old king's reign.

A change in royal line would normally result in a change of Dynasty but Tuthmosis I's legitimacy was reinforced by his marriage to Princess Ahmose, the daughter of Ahmose I and Queen Ahmose Nefertary.

Queen Hatshepsut's coup

At his death around 1518BC Tuthmosis I left behind a complicated succession situation. His two elder sons had predeceased him so his youngest son, also named Tuthmosis became heir. Tuthmosis II's mother was a minor royal and to strengthen Tuthmosis II's right as heir he was married to his half-sister, Hatshepsut.

Tuthmosis II died in his early thirties leaving behind a young son, Tuthmosis III, by Isis, a harem girl, and a daughter Neferure, by Hatshepsut. Tuthmosis II, seemingly aware of his wife's burning ambition, decreed before his death that his son, still a minor, should be his heir. As both his aunt and stepmother Hatshepsut acted as co-regent with the young Tuthmosis III but by the second year of the co-regency she had garnered support from senior officials, established herself as Queen in her own right and usurped the young king in the process.

To legitimise her claim as the rightful Queen she began building her splendid

ABOVE Amenhotep I depicted with his mother on a painted stele

OPPOSITE Massive osirian statues of Hatshepsut at the entrance to her tomb

mortuary temple in the bay of cliffs at Deir el-Bahari and recorded that she built the temple as a "garden for my father Amun". This was reinforced by a relief in the temple known as the "birth relief", a subtle piece of propaganda. The relief shows the god Amun visiting Hatshepsut's mother, Queen Ahmose and depicts nearby the appropriate deities of childbirth together with the seven "fairy Godmother" Hathors. This is intended to show that Hatshepsut had been deliberately conceived and chosen by Amun to be king and she is accordingly displayed with all the regalia of kingship, including the official royal false beard.

Reinforcing her status as king, Hatshepsut had her tomb dug in the Valley of Kings by her vizier and High Priest of Amun though an earlier tomb had been cut for her as queen regnant high up a cliff face in a remote valley west of the Valley of Kings.

Hatshepsut died in 1483BC after a reign of about 15 years, and there is a strong suspicion that Tuthmosis III, the usurped king kept so long in waiting, may have had a hand in her death. It is certainly clear that his destruction of her monuments and those of her closest followers indicates his hatred of her. Her greatest posthumous humiliation, though, was to be omitted from the carved king lists because her rule and the way she acquired it were felt to be too shameful to be recorded.

Egypt's Napoleon

During Hatshepsut's reign Tuthmosis III was kept very much in the background and it is assumed from the military successes achieved during reign in his own right that much of this time was spent training with the army.

The epithet "Egypt's Napoleon" was created by the American Egyptologist James Henry Breasted and is appropriate not just because of his military conquests but, also, his small stature, just over five feet. His reputation as a military campaigner is justified and his successes started in the second year of his independent reign with the spoils reaped from forays into Gaza and Yehem.

This was followed by 17 annual cam-

ABOVE Queen
Hatshepsut's temple
at Deir el-Bahri

OPPOSITE Statue
of Tuthmosis III in
the Luxor Museum

paigns of plunder against Western Asia, modern day Syria, with the Egyptian navy used for extensive troop movements up the coast.

Egypt's economy was enriched by the spoils from these ventures and many temples were endowed by gifts from Tuthmosis III, particularly the temple of Karnak, where wall reliefs represent some of the gold jewellery, furniture, precious oils and other goods provided by these gifts.

Tuthmosis lived into his eighties but had laid the groundwork for the greatest period of Egypt's wealth and influence overseen by his successors Amenhotep II, Tuthmosis IV and Amenhotep III.

The Amarna Interlude

Amenhotep III was succeeded in 1350BC by his second son Amenhotep IV, his first son having died prematurely. Amenhotep IV is better known as Akhenaten the name he assumed early in his reign, a reign which saw him introduce drastic changes to conventionally accepted religious beliefs and relocate his court and government to a brand new capital city, Akhetaten (modern day el-Armana). Historians refer to this period of radical change as the Armana Interlude.

It is clear that Akhenaten was much more of a thinker and philosopher than

his immediate predecessors and progressed even further the growing power of
the priesthood of Amun even though his
father, Amenhotep III had tried to curb
its growing and overwhelming influence.

Akhenaten instead increased the cult
of sun worship by introducing a new
monotheistic religion that was incar-
nate in the sun's disc, the Aten. In itself
this was not a new idea as the Aten, a
relatively minor aspect of the sun god
Re-Harakhte, had been venerated in the
Old Kingdom but Akhenaten's innova-
tion was to worship the Aten solely in
its own right.

To start his new initiative the king
built a temple to his god Aten just outside the east gate of the temple of Amun
at Karnak but conflict between the two
cults located so close together soon became apparent. Akhenaten resolved this
by proscribing the cult of Amun, closing
the god's temple and making over the
revenues to his own Aten cult. In year
six of his reign and to make the break
between Amun and Aten complete he
moved to a new capital in Middle Egypt,
halfway between Memphis and Thebes.
Built on a virgin site not previously
dedicated to any other deity, he called
his new city Akhetaten, translated as the
"Horizon of the Aten".

ABOVE Glass vase bearing the cartouche of Tuthmosis III

at Akhetaten the existing bureaucracy attempted to run the country in his absence. Cracks in the administration of Egypt may have started in the later years of Amenhotep III's reign but became much more evident as Akhenaten left government, diplomats and the army to their own devices.

Distracted by his philosophical and religious interests Akhenaten left the administration of Egypt to two powerful and closely related men, Ay, who held the title "Father of the God" and who it is thought was Akhenaten's father-in-law and Horemheb, a military general who was also Ay's son-in-law. Both these men would eventually become the final two kings of the 18th Dynasty following the premature death of Tutankhamun.

During Akhenaten's reign art underwent a noticeable change with, perhaps, a more accurate representation of the king's physical features. Pictures and statues of Akhenaten showing his protruding stomach, fat hips, pendulous breasts and long visage do not present a flattering picture though these features are also present, perhaps in deference to the king, in representations of other members of his court. Representations of Akhenaten's appearance may be accurate and the Egyptologist Bob Brier has suggested,

Akhetaten was only occupied during the reign of Akhenaten and present evidence suggest only the upper echelons of Egyptian society embraced the cult of Aten, but probably just in deference to the ruler and without any real conviction.

While Akhenaten courted his god

interestingly, that he may have suffered from Marfan's syndrome, a syndrome whose physical features closely mimic the appearance of Akhenaten.

Death of the boy-king

Nothing symbolises better our wonder and awe about ancient Egypt than the magnificent gold encrusted funerary artefacts recovered from Tutankhamun's tomb in 1922. In reality, Tutankhamun was a short lived and obscure king about which little was known, but with immortality now guaranteed by the contents of his almost intact tomb which had remained undisturbed for three thousand years following accidental concealment of its entrance just a few years after his death.

Though Tutankhamun's name was known from a few references discovered at the start of the 20th century his exact place in the sequence of the "Armana kings" was uncertain. Just like Akhenaten and Ay his name had been omitted from the classic king lists at Abydos and Karnak and until the detailed analysis of his mummy and DNA testing undertaken in recent years there was considerable conjecture about his exact identity and parentage.

ABOVE Akhenaten depicted as a sphinx at Akhentaten (modern day Amara)

Equally mysterious are the events surrounding his death with a long held suspicion he may have been murdered by his ambitious Chief Adviser, Ay. What is clear from forensic analysis of his mummy is that he died young, no older than 19, was frail, sickly and lame and probably walked with the aid of a cane.

Also clear is that without any offspring his death created a lacuna in the succession of the royal line with ambitious courtiers jostling for the role of king and putting his young widow, Queen Ankhesenamun, in a very difficult position. Feeling oppressed and threatened by

powerful men much older than herself she took the unprecedented step of writing to Suppilulimius I, king of the Hittites, explaining her plight, that her husband had died and she had no sons while he had many and could he send one to marry her and continue the royal line.

Though initially suspicious, Suppilulimius I made the appropriate enquiries and then despatched a Hittite prince, Zannanza to Egypt to take up Ankhesenamun's offer. Zannanza got as far as the border of Egypt and was then promptly murdered, almost certainly at the command of Horemheb who as commander-in-chief of the army had the means, the opportunity and, more particularly, the motive.

Succession was finally resolved when Ay, already an old man, became king by marrying Ankhesenamun who was almost certainly coerced unwillingly into a match she had been trying to avoid, particularly as it meant she was actually marrying her grandfather.

Ay's reign was brief, just four years, and he was succeeded by Horemheb who became the last king of the 18th Dynasty. Though a powerful man Horemheb was a commoner by birth but justified his claim to the throne by his marriage to Mutnodjme who, as the sister of Nefertiti, enabled him to claim continuity of the female royal blood line.

Ramesses the Great

In some respects it is hard to explain why Manetho showed the 18th Dynasty seguing into the 19th Dynasty after the death of Horemheb as the change in royal line and ruling family arguably occurred with the death of Tutankhamun.

The 19th Dynasty started in a low key way, its first ruler Ramesses I, Horemheb's vizier, friend and confidant, assuming the rule when Horemheb died without any heirs. Ramesses I, a career army officer, was not of royal blood but was succeeded after a short two year reign by his son Seti I. To restore Egyptian fortunes following the instability of the Armana period Seti I started a major building programme, established a strategic foreign policy and, to legitimatise the new era, took the time honoured additional title of "Repeater of births".

Seti I ruled for about 13 years but it was his son, Ramesses II, who really

established the character and profile of the 19th Dynasty. Ruling for 67 years his popular title "Ramesses the Great" can be attributed to his military victories, the size and number of temples and statues he constructed and last, but not least, the enormous number of children he sired.

His military campaigns sought to recover territories in the Levant held by the 18th Dynasty and culminated in the Battle of Kadesh waged against the Hittite king Mu-watalli II.

His immediate successors continued the military campaigns but with decreasing effectiveness associated with troubled court politics. These included a break in the royal line when the king's role was usurped by Amenmesses, an unknown and shadowy king, and the end of the dynasty triggered by the death of Siptah without heirs and the assumption of his role by his stepmother Queen Twosret who ruled for a brief two years.

OPPOSITE
The mummy of Tutankhamun stripped of its jewels and finery

LEFT TOP
Tutankhamun receives flowers from his wife Ankhesenamun, from the lid of a box found in his tomb

LEFT BOTTOM
Head of Ramesses II from one of the four massive seated statues at Abu Simbel

ABOVE Egyptians fighting the Sea People at the battle of Djahy

OPPOSITE Map showing the Egyptian and Hittite kingdoms at the time of the Battle of Kadesh

Decline and fall

Little is known about Setnakhte, the first ruler of the 20th Dynasty and his brief, three year reign. He may have been remotely related to the Ramesside royal family or may have usurped the role from Queen Twosret. He certainly usurped the tomb that had been prepared for her.

The most famous pharaoh of the 20th Dynasty is Ramesses III who during the 30 years of his reign had to contend with sporadic invasions into the Delta region and an attack by an enemy described as the Sea Peoples by the Egyptians. The term Sea Peoples appears to embrace a confederacy of seafaring raiders made up of people from western Anatolia (modern day Asian Turkey) and southern Europe from around the Aegean Sea. Before attacking Egypt the Sea Peoples had successfully invaded Syria, Canaan and Cyprus.

Attacks by Libyans on the Delta region and invasion by the Sea Peoples may have been related to a period of drought and consequent shortage of food. Certainly during the last 50 or so years of the Dynasty and a series of kings all named Ramesses, Egypt suffered drought, famine and grumbling dissent from hungry workers. Loss of central administrative control again saw local power in both Upper and Lower Egypt ranged against each other and by the time of the Dynasty's last king, Ramesses XI, and a state of near civil war it was no longer possible for him to travel throughout the country in safety.

Weakened by wars, famine and civil unrest and now economically bankrupt this was the point that marked the end of the 20th Dynasty, the end of the New Kingdom with Egypt again slipping into a period of fragmented control and political uncertainty referred to by historians as the Third Intermediate Period.

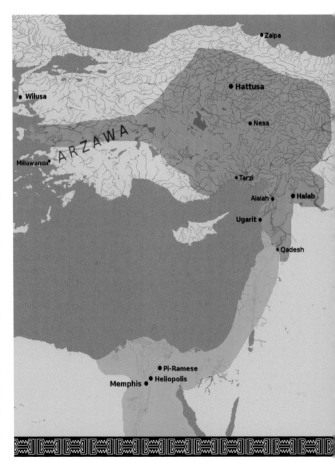

Chapter 10

DISCOVERING TUTANKHAMUN'S TOMB

OPPOSITE LEFT
Howard Carter, discoverer of Tutankhamun's tomb

OPPOSITE RIGHT
Tutankhamun's magnificent gold funerary mask

For ever linked with Tutankhamun's tomb and almost as famous was its discoverer Howard Carter. Born in 1874 he became involved in Egypt's antiquities at an early age and spent a season digging at Armana under the tutelage of Flinders Petrie followed by five years (1894 – 99) working with Edouard Naville at Deir el-Bahari, where he recorded the wall reliefs in the temple of Hatshepsut. His next five years were spent as the first Chief Inspector of the Egyptian Antiquities Service (EAS) and from 1907 he was employed supervising Lord Carnarvon's excavations in the Valley of the Kings.

Apart from a three year interruption during World War I, Lord Carnarvon financed Carter's work through to 1922 though by then the level of discoveries and recovered artefacts had become a disappointment to Lord Carnarvon. From discoveries dating back to the start of the century Carter felt sure that Tutankhamun's tomb was in the Valley of the Kings but in 1922 Lord Carnarvon advised Carter he had one more season to find Tutankhamun's tomb before funding would be withdrawn.

Fate stepped in and on the 4th November 1922 Carter's team found steps that Carter hoped would lead to

Tutankhamun's tomb. His suspicions were correct, he wired Lord Carnarvon and on the 26th November 1922 accompanied by Carnarvon, Carnarvon's daughter and other officials, Carter made a "tiny breach in the top left-hand corner" of the tomb's doorway. Peering in he could see that many of the gold and ebony treasures were still intact and when asked by Carnarvon "Can you see anything?" replied with the now famous words "Yes, wonderful things".

A second-hand tomb?

Behind the tomb's door a sloping corridor led down to two sealed cham-

ABOVE A scarab decorated pectoral belonging to Tutankhamun

bers, the Annexe on the left and the burial chamber on the right. The burial chamber was almost completely filled with the huge catafalque of four gold overlaid wooden shrines enclosing Tutankhamun's red quartzite sarcophagus with its cracked granite lid. Of the nest of three coffins in the sarcophagus the innermost was of solid gold bearing the now world famous solid gold funerary mask while the outer two were made of wood overlaid with gold.

Tutankhamun's gold mask weighed 22½ lbs (10.23kg) and the solid gold coffin weighed 243 lbs (110.4kg) but amidst all this splendour the king's mortal remains struck a pitiful contrast, the result of poor and hasty embalming.

The artistic magnificence of the mask and gold coffin suggest these were prepared well in advance of Tutankhamun's death but other aspects of the tomb suggest an unexpected death and a hasty burial. Many of the funerary artefacts appear to have "come from stock" while others appear to have been prepared for other members of the royal family. The tomb too, with its cramped contents, was far too small for a royal burial and was not Tutankhamun's original intended burial place. His intended tomb is now believed to be one discovered in 1816 at the western end of the Valley of the Kings by Giovanni Belzoni and used instead by Ay, the court official once suspected by some of murdering Tutankhamun.

For a long time Tutankhamun's place in the royal lineage remained a mystery and with his name omitted from the principal king lists there was conjecture about his parentage. From relics in his tomb it was clear that he had been brought up at Amarna, probably in the North Palace, suggesting there must have been some relationship with Akhenaten.

Since 2005 intensive forensic analysis of Tutankhamun's remains have resolved the problem of parentage but raised a host of other questions regarding his

BELOW Tomb of Tutankhamun

ABOVE
Egyptian chariot

How did he die?

For a long time there was compelling though circumstantial evidence that Tutankhamun was murdered but from the ongoing forensic analysis the general consensus now is that his death was an accident. Scientists have interpreted the evidence in different ways and though he seems to have been quite sickly, suffering from endemic malaria and foot deformations probably related to his genetic inheritance, his actual death seems to have been the result of traumatic injuries on the left side of his body incurred, perhaps, in an accident such as a chariot crash.

The most intriguing research supporting this theory was a virtual autopsy performed at the end of 2013 by Egyptologist Dr Chris Naunton of Britain's Cranfield Institute working in conjunction with car-crash investigators. From computer simulations of chariot crashes Dr Naunton concluded that Tutankhamun was in fact mortally wounded in a chariot crash. Thrown from his own chariot a second chariot smashed into him while he was on his knees, shattering his ribs and pelvis though the evidence of infection in his

actual cause of death. In 2008 a team began DNA research on Tutankhamun and the mummified remains of other family members. Though still incomplete the research to date has confirmed that he was the son of Akhenaten though his mother was none of Akhenaten's known wives but was, instead, one of his father's five sisters which, with inbred defects, may go some way to explaining his frail physiology.

fractured left leg suggests he may have survived for some days following the crash.

The truth about the curse

The idea of a mummy's curse was largely created by the media following the apparently mysterious deaths of some members of Howard Carter's team. In fact the only significant time sensitive death was that of Lord Carnarvon. A few weeks after the discovery of the tomb he was bitten by a mosquito, knicked it while shaving and died of blood poising two weeks later following infection of the cut.

A newspaper report shortly after his death confidently asserted hieroglyphs in Tutankhamun's tomb spelled out "Death shall come on swift wings to him who disturbs the peace of the King" and seems to have been the catalyst for a media frenzy that associated the curse with even the deaths of people only vaguely connected with the tomb's discovery. But the curse is a complete fiction and nothing remotely like its words have ever been found anywhere in Tutankhamun's tomb.

Howard Carter was always sceptical of

PEER LEAPS 100 FT. TO DEATH
Could Not Stand Any More Horrors
TOMB INSCRIPTIONS THREATEN VENGEANCE

LONDON, February 22 1930

"I really cannot stand any more horrors," he said in a letter written before he jumped to his death 100 ft. from the seventh floor of his flat in St. James' Court.

Source: SAFF

ABOVE Sensational newspaper headline from 1930

such curses and a 1930s study showed that of the 58 people present when the tomb was opened, six had since died, a number, considering their ages in 1922, within the normal statistical range.

Chapter 11

THE THIRD INTERMEDIATE PERIOD

The Third Intermediate Period started with control of Egypt split between secular kings ruling the south from their Delta stronghold while the north was firmly in the hands of priests based at Thebes.

This division of power persisted for over a hundred years and set a pattern that was to persist for the next half millennium. Power and influence in the country became increasingly fragmented with contemporaneous and overlapping Dynasties having control in different regions and with some of those Dynasties a sequence of foreign kings from Libya, Assyria and Nubia.

This implies 500 years of turmoil but in practice there were long periods of stability and peaceable co-existence between the regions while most ordinary Egyptians living in their own region would have seen little change in their day to day life.

For two thousand years Egypt had been the pre-eminent ancient civilisation both powerful and rich. But by 1000BC it was virtually bankrupt and the next thousand years saw it lose influence as it became just another Mediterranean civilisation, sometimes entering into battle with its neighbours but just as likely to engage in trade as well as diplomatic and cultural exchange.

Greater involvement in the wider Mediterranean and Near East region culminated in 525BC with the Persian conquest of Egypt, the event regarded as marking the end of The Third Intermediate Period.

Dynasty	Period BC	Pharaohs
High Priests (at Thebes)	1080 - 945	Heribor
		Piankh
		Pinedjem
		Masaherta
		Menkeperre
		Smendes II
		Pinedjem II
		Psusennes III
21	1069 - 945	Smendes II
		Amenemnisu
		Psusennes I
		Amenemope
		Osorkon the Elder
		Siamun
		Psusennes II
22 At Tanis	945 - 712	Sheshonq I
		Osorkon I
		Sheshonq II
		Takelot I
		Osorkon II
		Takelot II
		Shesonq III
		Pami
		Shesonq V
		Osorkon IV
At Thebes	870 - 860	Harsiese
23	818 - 715	Pedibastet
At Leontopolis		Shesonq IV
		Osorkon III
		Takelot III

Continued:

Dynasty	Period BC	Pharaohs
		Rudamon
		Iuput
At Heakleopolis		Peftjauabastet
At Hermopolis		Nimlot
24	727 - 715	Tefnakht
At Sais		Bakenrenef
25	747 - 656	Piankhi
		Shabaka
		Shebitku
		Taharqa
		Tanutamun
26	664 - 525	Psamtik I
At Saite		Nekau
		Psamtik II
		Wahibre
		Ahmose II
		Psamtik III

The 21st Dynasty and Theban priests

Though based at Thebes the priesthood of Amun had immense countrywide power. It owned two-thirds

of all temple land in Egypt, 90% of all ships and 80% of all factories together with many other properties. Exercise of their power crystallised in 1080 BC, ten years before the death of Ramesses XI, when Herihor established a Dynasty of High Priest at Thebes controlling Upper and Middle Egypt and enforcing supremacy over the Ramesside Dynasty.

Herihor's antecedents are unknown but it is believed his wife, Nodjmet, was the sister of Ramesses XI and a continued pattern of marriage between the ruling families of the two parallel Dynasties ensured the maintenance of a reasonable relationship.

The founding of cities in the eastern Delta by kings of the 19th and 20th Dynasties and the location of power there had reinforced the split between Upper and Lower Egypt and though the priests at Thebes paid lip service to the Delta kings no one was in any doubt about who controlled Upper Egypt.

Following the death of Ramesses XI in 1070, Smendes proclaimed himself king and his rule marks the start of the 21st Dynasty. His origins are obscure but marriage to one of Ramesses XI's daughters seems to justify his claim to the royal line.

During Smendes reign he moved the ruling Delta capital from Piramesse to Tanis and the Dynasty's stone-built burial chambers were found there in a temple dedicated to the Theban gods Amun, Mut and Khonsu. It was there that in 1939-40 the archaeologist Pierre Montet discovered the only ever completely intact pharaonic tomb (Tutankhamun's had been robbed twice in antiquity and then resealed before the entrance was accidentally concealed). This belonged to Psusennes, the third king of the 21st Dynasty, and included a fine gold funerary mask but not one that bears comparison with Tutankhamun's.

The 22nd and 23rd Dynasties

The 22nd Dynasty, referred to as the Libyan or Bubastite Dynasty, was founded in 945BC by Sheshonq I, a descendant of Meshwesh immigrants from ancient Libya. Sheshonq I successfully reunited the country and inaugurated a sequence of Libyan kings who would rule Egypt for the next 200 years. United stability persisted for over a hundred years but after the reign of Osorkon II control again fractured into two with Takelot II and his son Osorkon (Osorkon III of the 23rd Dynasty) ruling Middle and Upper Egypt while Sheshonq III continued to control Lower Egypt from the Delta region.

In Thebes a civil war started when a prince called Pedibastet challenged Takelot II and his son Osorkon for control of Upper and Middle Egypt. Pedibastet proclaimed a new Dynasty, the 23rd, with himself as the founding king. The 23rd Dynasty was relatively short lived and quickly fragmented after the death of Rudamon in 754BC to be replaced by local city states under the control of separate local kings, Peftjauabastet at Herakleopolis, Nimlot at Hermopolis and Ini at Thebes.

The 24th Dynasty

During the second half of the 8th century BC the Nubian kingdom to the south took full advantage of the political insta-

OPPOSITE A map that demonstrates the fragmentation of power in Egypt at the start of the Third Intermediate Period

ABOVE Ruins of the city of Tanis today in Egypt at the start of the Third Intermediate Period

BELOW King Tefnakht portrayed on his eight year stele

RIGHT Pendant bearing the cartouche of 22nd Dynasty King Osorkon II

bility in Upper Egypt. The Nubian ruler Kashta was able to extend his influence over Thebes and there he compelled Takelot III's sister, the serving Divine Adoratice of Amun, to adopt his own daughter Amenirdis to be her successor.

In response to further Nubian incursions by Piankhi, Kashta's successor, the short lived 24th Dynasty was founded in 727BC to try and regain Egyptian control of Upper Egypt. Its founding ruler, Tefnakht, based in the Delta, was successful in forming a confederation of northern kings and city state rulers that included Osorkon IV, Peftjauabastet, Nimlot and Iuput.

The confederation of northern rulers achieved some initial successes but after the opposing forces met at Herakleopolis Tefnakht was forced to retreat to Hermopolis where he and the other confederation kings surrendered to the Nubian king Piankhi. Piankhi then established A Nubian 25th Dynasty and appointed all four confederation "kings" as governors of their regions.

Tefnacht's reign lasted for about eight years and he was succeeded by Bakenrenef, the second and only other king of the 24th Dynasty, whose reign lasted for six years.

The 25th Dynasty

Having established the 25th Dynasty the Nubian king Piankhi was successful in restoring a united Egypt. He was succeeded by his brother Shabaka and then by his two sons Shebitku and Taharqa.

The newly reunited Nile Valley Empire was as large as it had been since the New Kingdom. Pharaohs such as Shebitku and Taharqa built and restored temples and monuments throughout the Nile, including at Memphis, Karnak, Kawa and Jebel Barkal.

Egypt's prestige had declined considerably by this time and many of its allies and neighbours had fallen under the influence of and were in thrall to Assyria. By the beginning of the 7th century BC the question was for how long war between Egypt and Assyria could be avoided. Despite Egypt's size and wealth

Assyria had an ample supply of timber compared to Egypt's chronic shortage, providing Assyria with a ready supply of charcoal for iron smelting and the production of weapons.

This critical advantage became apparent when Assyria invaded Egypt in 670BC. From then on Pharaoh Taharqa's reign and, later, that of his cousin Tanutamun was occupied with constant conflict with the Assyrians culminating in a mortal blow in 664BC when they attacked and sacked Thebes and Memphis.

This event brought the 25th Dynasty to a close and its Nubian rulers eventually retreated to Napata at the southern border of Egypt with Nubia. It was there, at El-Kurru and Nuri that all 25th Dynasty pharaohs are buried under the first pyramids built in the Nile valley for hundreds of years. The relocated Dynasty, styled the Na-

LEFT Taharqa presented in the guise of a sphinx

BELOW Head of Tantamum, last Nubian (Kushite) King of the 25th Dynasty

ABOVE Kushite
pyramids at Nuri,
near Jebel Barkal

OPPOSITE TOP
Meeting between
Cambyses II and
Psamtik III at
Pelusium

OPPOSITE BOTTOM
Cambyses II capturing
pharaoh Samtik III after
his conquest of Egypt
in 525 BC

patan Dynasty, led to the establishment of the Kingdom of Kush which flourished at Napata and Meroe, surviving up to the 2nd century AD.

End of the Third Intermediate Period

For a time Upper Egypt remained under the rule of Tanutamun but from 664BC Lower Egypt was ruled by the 26th Dynasty, puppet kings installed by the Assyrians but who nonetheless secured political independence at a time when the Assyrian Empire was facing its own troubles.

In 656BC Psamtik I, the Dynasty's first king, occupied Thebes, becoming ruler of Upper and Lower Egypt, reuniting the country and bringing increased stability to the country during his 54 year long reign from the Delta city of Sais.

Four successive Saite kings continued guiding Egypt towards peace and prosperity but unfortunately this stability was brusquely interrupted by the growth of a new power in the Near East – Persia.

Psamtik III had succeeded his father, Ahmose II, for only six months when in 525BC he was forced into a confrontation with the Persian army at Pelusium.

The Egyptian army was no match for the Persians who had already attacked and conquered Babylon. Psamtik III was defeated and although he escaped to Memphis he was soon captured, imprisoned and later executed at Susa, the capital of the Persian king Cambyses who then assumed the formal title of Pharaoh of Egypt.

Chapter 12

THE LATE PERIOD

BELOW Cambyses II

For the last five hundred years of the BC era, before the birth of Christ, the Mediterranean was awhirl with newer civilisations jostling for control of the region's territories and rich resources: the Assyrians, Persians, Macedonians, Greeks and Romans but not the Egyptians.

Instead Egypt, with its fertile valley and material resources, was a target for expanding empires and apart from a brief half-century interlude in the 4th century BC, Egypt was ruled by foreign conquerors starting with the Persian invasion of 525BC through to the Roman invasion of 30BC. In chronological terms the Roman's invasion of Egypt in 30BC is generally regarded as the date marking the end of ancient Egyptian civilisation.

Whether in honour, as homage or just to appease the indigenous population the foreign invaders adopted much of Egypt's culture including dress, religion and architectural traditions. The Hellenic invaders, Egypt's Ptolemaic Dynasty, even embraced the practice of siblings marrying each other.

For Egypt this final five hundred years seems like a slow decline from the earlier eras of such magnificence but at least the invasion by Alexander the Great and the establishment of Alexandria brought Egypt fully into the intellectual orbit of the modern Mediterranean world.

The Persian Conquest

Kings of the 26th Dynasty had successfully restored old values, reunited the country and reinvigorated its central administration.

Dynasty	Period BC	Pharaohs
27 First Persian Period	525 - 404	Cambyses II Darius I Xerxes Darius II Artaxerxes II
Egyptian interlude 28	404 -399	Amyrtaeus
29	399 - 380	Nefaarud I Hakor
30	380 - 343	Nakhtnebet Djedhor Nakhthoreb
31 Second Persian Period		Artaxerxes III Arses Darius III
Macedonian Kings	332 - 305	Alexander the Great Philip Arrhidaeus Alexander IV
Ptolemaic Dynasty	305 - 30	Ptolemy I Soter Ptolemy II Philadelphus Ptolemy III Euergetes Ptolemy IV Philopator Ptolemy V Epiphanes Ptolemy VI Philometor Ptolemy VII Neos Philopator Ptolemy VIII Euregetes II Ptolemy IX Soter II Ptolemy X Alexander I Ptolemy X1 Alexander II Ptolemy XII Neos Dionysos Queen Berenice IV Queen Cleopatra VII Ptolemy XV Caesarion

When the Persian king Cambyses II defeated Psamtik III, the last king of the 26th Dynasty, he merely had to assume control of a well administered realm.

History reports that after his initial victory over Egypt he had few further military successes with legends of him losing an entire army in the desert. The story is probably apocryphal but within three years of his Egyptian conquest he was dead and although he had his name written in a cartouche he remained a Persian and was buried at Takht-i-Rustam, near Persepolis.

Like absentee landlords, Cambyses II and the other kings of the Persian Dynasty, the 27th Dynasty, ruled Egypt from the Persian capital Susa, leaving management of the country in the hands of a series of satraps, some of whom acquired reputations for being particularly cruel.

Cambyses II was succeeded in 522BC by Darius I who, in a long 35 year reign, took much greater interest, curtailed the excesses of the worst satraps and engaged in a building programme. This included the repair of temples from Busiris in the Delta region to El-Kab in the south, just north of Aswan, as well as building a new temple at Khargah Oasis. In addition he completed a canal from Pelusium, on the eastern Delta, to the Red Sea which had been started by Nekau in the 26th Dynasty.

During the 120 year Persian reign there were occasional revolts by the indigenous population, including a revolt in 486BC when the Persians were distracted by long running wars with the Greeks. With the aid sometimes of Greek mercenaries occasional revolts continued over the next 30 years until the capture and execution in 454BC of Prince Inures of Heliopolis, one of the leading Egyptian campaigners.

Following the death of Darius II in 405BC Amyrtaeus, Prince of Sais, who for six years had fought a guerrilla campaign against the Persians, declared himself pharaoh and was able to assert his authority as far south as Aswan. Virtually nothing is known about Amyrtaeus who ruled for five years and was the sole king of the 28th Dynasty.

LEFT Sphinx
of King Hakor

The Egyptians back in power

Egyptian rule was sustained by the 29th Dynasty and its founder Nefaarud I. Little is known about him but he relocated the royal capital from Sais to more centrally located Mendes suggesting, perhaps, a closer connection with the royal line of that city. In any event there is evidence during his short six year reign of building work and inscriptions that link him back to the Saite policies of the 26th Dynasty.

Following his death in 393BC there was a year of confusion over his succession and his son and another rival were eventually overcome by an unrelated man, Hakor (Achoris) who tried to create the impression of a legitimate relationship with Nefaarud I with inscriptions on monuments and by naming his own son Nefaarud.

During his 14 year reign Hakor undertook an enormous amount of building, rebuilding and refurbishing as well as demonstrating flair for Mediterranean politics by establishing alliances with the Greeks.

Fights over succession seem to have been a feature of this last period of Egyptian rule and Hakor's son was ousted by Nakhtnebef, the founder of the 30th Dynasty and the last Dynasty of Egyptian rulers.

The reigns of Nakhtnebef and his grandson Nakhthoreb were characterised by the restoration of dilapidated temples and a return to the old values and stability provided by the traditional Egyptian gods. While this work was being undertaken the 30th Dynasty faced little threat from the Persians who were preoccupied with external and internal threats to their own empire.

But by 350BC the new Persian ruler, Artaxerxes III, had sufficiently re-established authority over his domain to contemplate re-attacking Egypt. Initial forays failed but in 343BC Nakhthoreb and an army of 100,000 men, including

RIGHT TOP Sphinx of 30th Dynasty King Nakhtnebef

RIGHT BOTTOM A relief of Artaxerxes on his tomb ar Persepolis

20,000 Greek mercenaries, found themselves facing the latest Persian advance at Pelusium, Egypt's fortress entrance on the eastern Delta. The Persian army was also reinforced with Greek mercenaries who demonstrating better tactics were able to outflank the Egyptians. Pelusium fell followed by other Delta cities and Memphis. Nakhthoreb fled south, seeking refuge in Nubia, but what happened to him after that is unknown today.

Persian rule was again established in Egypt and the 30th Dynasty came to an end with Nakhthoreb being the last ever Egyptian pharaoh. Egypt would not have another native Egyptian leader for over 2,000 years and the appointment of Mohamed Naguib as Egypt's first president after the July 1952 Revolution.

The return of the Persians

In contrast to the length of the first Persian Dynasty, this second Dynasty, the 31st, was short lived, just over 10 years, with little evidence of Persian influence during that period.

The Persians had their own problems. Artaxerxes III was poisoned in Persia in 338BC, his young successor, Arses ruled for only two years before being murdered and succeeded by Darius III.

This was the era of Alexander the Great (Alexander III), installed as the king of Macedonia in 336BC at the age of 20 following the assassination of his father, Philip II. In 334BC Alexander launched a campaign against the Persian Empire, successfully conquering Asia Minor, the Levant and Syria, reaching Egypt by the end of 332BC. Darius III who had already lost in earlier encounters with Alexander wisely ordered the surrender of Egypt, saving the country and, ultimately, his own skin.

The Macedonian Kings

After another uncomfortable period being ruled by a Persian satrapy the Egyptians regarded Alexander the Great as their liberator, pronouncing him the new "Master of the Universe" and son of Amun at the Oracle of Siwa Oasis in the Libyan Desert. From then on Alexander often referred to Zeus-Ammon as his true father and subsequent currency depicted him adorned with ram's horns as a symbol of his divinity.

During his short stay in Egypt Alexander founded the city Alexandra which would become the prosperous capital of ancient Egypt's final Ptolemaic Dynasty. Alexander left Egypt in 331BC to continue his campaign against the Persians and never

returned between then and his death in 323BC. Instead he carried on ruling Egypt in the same way as the Persians, by appointing a satrap capable of ruling Egypt with its existing administrative structure.

History records two other Macedonian kings ruling Egypt, Philip Arrhidaeus from 323 – 317BC and Alexander IV from 317 – 305BC although in fact he had been murdered in 311BC. Throughout this period the real ruler and de-facto king was the Hellenic satrap Ptolemy.

Following Alexander's death and the eventual breakup of his empire, his generals, known as the *diadochi* (followers) pursued their independent interests while Ptolemy moved to Egypt and strengthened his position, being answerable only to the Council of State set up in Babylon after Alexander's death.

ABOVE Mosaic detail representing Alexander the Great on his horse Bucephalus

BELOW The Ptolemaic Empire in 200BC

RIGHT Bust of Ptolemy I Soter

Ptolemy proved himself an astute operator and while Alexander the Great's body was en route from Babylon to its final resting place in Macedonia he kidnapped it, recognising how symbolically important it was to the Egyptian people. Although Alexander's tomb was originally intended to be in Memphis the actual site was in Alexandria, at a site now believed to be under the sea.

By 305BC Ptolemy was sufficiently secure and confident to pronounce himself Pharaoh and founded the last great Egyptian Dynasty, the Ptolemaic Dynasty, which was to last for almost 300 years.

The Ptolemaic Dynasty

By establishing the Ptolemaic Kingdom Ptolemy I Sozer created a powerful Hellenistic dynasty that ruled an area stretching from southern Syria to Cyrene and south to Nubia. In the greater Ptolemaic kingdom the Ptolemaics were powerful monarchs but in Egypt they cleverly continued the line of god-kings, honouring the prominent priesthood that, with an excellent civil service, kept the country stable and prosperous. The Ptolemies and their queens appeared on coinage in royal Hellenistic style while in Egypt they appeared on temple reliefs with full pharaonic trappings in the traditional Egyptian style.

During the reign of Ptolemy I a start was made on many vast building projects

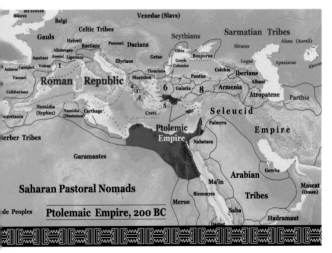

Ptolemaic Empire, 200 BC

of temples and towns that would continue throughout the Dynasty. These included the Pharos lighthouse, one of the seven Wonders of the Ancient World and the Library at Alexandria that became one of the greatest centres of learning in the old World.

Today the finest extant temples in Egypt belong to the Ptolemaic period, temples such as Dendara, Edfu and Philae. Many of them were built exactly on the footprint of earlier temples which makes it difficult for archaeologists to determine exactly the chronological sequence of building.

All the male rulers of the Dynasty took the name Ptolemy while princesses and queens favoured the names Cleopatra, Arsinoe and Berenice. Because the Ptolemaic kings adopted the old Egyptian custom of marrying their sisters many of the kings ruled jointly with their spouses who were of the same royal house. This custom made Ptolemaic politics confusingly incestuous and later generations of Ptolemaics became increasingly enfeebled with evermore internecine warfare between brothers, sisters and cousins.

From around 200BC Rome began annexing territories and expanding its sphere of influence. The growth of Rome and eventual establishment of an Empire coincided with the decline of the Ptolemaic Dynasty whose indulgent rulers were increasingly despised by the Egyptian population. To maintain the Dynasty the Ptolemies allied themselves with the Romans in a pact that lasted over 150 years but which also saw the Romans gaining ever more power over Egypt with Cleopatra's (Cleopatra VII)

ABOVE LEFT Ring with the engraved head of Ptolemy VI Philometor in Egyptian headwear

ABOVE RIGHT Corinthian pillar from the Ptolemaic period

BELOW Relief of
Cleopatra and her son
Ptolemy XV Caesarion
at the temple of
Dendara

RIGHT Bust of
Cleopatra at Altes
Museum, Berlin

father Ptolemy XII, having to pay a tribute, a sort of protection payment, to keep them out of his kingdom.

Cleopatra, a femme fatale

Countless plays, novels and films have confirmed Cleopatra as one of history's most iconic and alluring characters with her real life sometimes even more dramatic than its artistic portrayal.

Following Ptolemy XII's death in 51BC Egypt was bequeathed to her at the age of 17 with the injunction that she must marry the elder of her two brothers, Ptolemy XIII. He, with the aid of two scheming courtiers, Pothinus and Achillas, attempted to murder her, but receiving a warning she escaped to exile in Syria.

She soon returned with an army and confronted her brother in a stand-off at Pelusium, neither side being prepared to make a move. At this point Julius Caser entered the scene, pursuing his defeated adversary Pompey after the 48BC battle of Pharsalus. Pompey, hoping for sanctuary

with Ptolemy XIII landed at Pelusium where he was promptly murdered by the court conspirators Pothinus and Achillas.

Pompey's severed head was presented to Caesar when he arrived at Alexandria and, ever ruthless, he immediately had Pothinus executed. He then summoned the young queen and her brother and chose to give his support to Cleopatra. Ptolemy XIII together with Achillas fought back with a siege of the Romans on Pharos Island but was drowned in the attempt.

To keep the necessary co-ruling status Cleopatra then married her younger brother Ptolemy XIV but at the same time became Caesar's mistress and later bore him a son, Ptolemy XV Caesarion, the last recorded king, as Cleopatra's co-regent, of the Ptolemaic Dynasty.

Seeing Cleopatra, still a young woman, picking her way through this political minefield it is clear that, though noted for her beauty, she was, more importantly, intelligent and very astute. She was, apparently, the only one of the Ptolemies capable of understanding and speaking Egyptian.

Caesar's death resulted in a struggle for power between Octavian and Mark Antony which culminated in a sea battle at Actium on the west coast of Greece on the 2nd September 31BC. There was no quick decisive victory but suddenly for some unaccountable reason, mutiny or misunderstood orders, Antony broke off the engagement and sailed for open sea, following Cleopatra's ships back to Egypt.

A year later Octavian resumed the fight, entering Alexandria on the 1st August 30BC. In a now well reprised lovers tryst Cleopatra committed suicide while Antony fell on his sword. Octavian had them buried together in the royal mausoleum in the Sema at Alexandria that Cleopatra had prepared to receive her body.

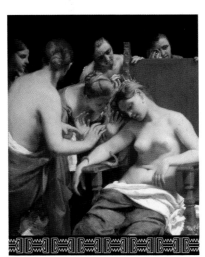

ABOVE Battle of Actium by Lorenzo A Castro 1672

LEFT The death of Cleopatra by Guido Cagnacci 1658

Chapter 13

ROMAN EGYPT

RIGHT Roman amphitheatre in Alexandria

Although Rome conquered Egypt with the defeat of Antony and Cleopatra the country did not follow the normal template for a Roman province. Instead Octavian, who had become Augustus in 27BC and the first emperor of Rome, treated Egypt as his own personal estate. It was ruled by a prefect, answerable to the emperor and no member of the imperial family or the Senate was allowed to visit Egypt without the express approval of Augustus.

Just like other foreign rulers, Augustus and successive emperors maintained the Pharaonic fiction, appearing in Egyptian dress and headwear on reliefs and statues and adhering to the old religious rituals.

Roman Egypt was immensely prosperous and many new cities were built with all the classic Roman buildings such as baths, basilica and agora. New temples were also built, many of them built to old established patterns. The temple at Esna, for example, matches the layout of the earlier Ptolemaic temple at Dendara and features several 1st century AD emperors in reliefs on its walls.

Much of Egypt's prosperity was related to the production of vast quantities of grain, an important factor in the maintenance of stability in Rome. The famous Juvenal quotation about keeping the mob happy captures that very accurately – "Give them bread and circuses". The Coliseum was the circus and the bread was provided by the grain fleet that sailed from Alexandria every year.

Chapter 14

SOME RECENT DISCOVERIES

BELOW Map showing the location of the sunken port and city Heracleion

OPPOSITE LEFT Ptolemaic coins recoverd from Heracleion

OPPOSITE RIGHT The stele of Ptolemy VIII recovered from the sunken temple of Heracleion

If you are interested in keeping abreast of the latest discoveries and revelations about ancient Egypt it is worth tracking the internet on a regular basis.

Every year, no, every month, there are new discoveries, from newly revealed tombs and excavated artefacts to revised analysis of museum treasures that add more pieces to the 5,000 year old jigsaw and now the exciting finds revealed by the use of modern scientific techniques such as CAT scanning and DNA testing.

Here are just three recent discoveries that add to our knowledge and experience of ancient Egypt

The ancient port of Heracleion

Though not now a particularly recent find, the discovery of the submerged port of Heracleion in 2001 was one of this century's most important finds and one which will keep archaeologists busy for decades to come.

Archaeologists have been able to establish that the port, which is now 2.5km from land, dates back to 1200BC, the era of the New Kingdom and that it was particularly important during the 4th and 5th centuries BC until eclipsed around 300BC by the new port and capital, Alexandria, established by Alexander the Great in 332BC. It is thought

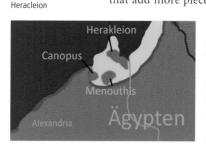

the port and city sank below the waves around 700AD, perhaps as the result of an earthquake, which has left some historians wondering if the event might be the source of the Atlantis myth.

As well as the remains of an amazing 64 ships the site also includes the temple of Amun-Gereb, dozens of sarcophagi, enormous statues, including ones of the goddess Isis and the god Hapi, as well as many steles inscribed, like the Rosetta Stone, in hieroglyphics, Greek and .Egyptian demotic script.

Revealing mummies secrets with CT scans

The British Museum acquired its first mummy in 1756 and now has 120 though none have been unwrapped for the last 200 years which means that very little, not even their gender, is known about them.

RIGHT CAT scan of Gebelan man, Predynastic period, about 3500BC

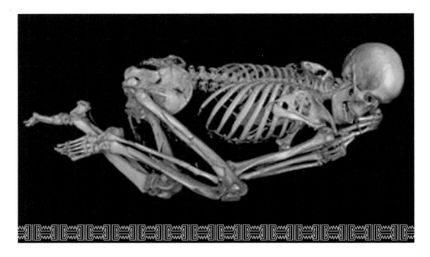

In November 2013 the Museum opened a free exhibition which presents the results of CT scans performed on eight of the mummies in its collection. The eight, including two children, range in age from 700 AD to 3500BC allowed visitors to see faces whose hair and flesh has survived thousands of years thanks to either artificial mummification or naturally through burial in the hot, dry sands of the Nile Valley desert.

Curator Dr John Taylor of the Museum says "It's very new technology, cutting-edge stuff, and we couldn't have done this even five years ago. We can peel away layers, remove the skin, go inside the body and look at the body from every angle with immense clarity. We want people to see them and recognise them as human beings. Some of the faces are astonishingly well-preserved."

Twin tombs

Beginning in the 19th century, tourist trips to visit the antiquities of Egypt have grown enormously in popularity though since the Arab Spring Revolu-

LEFT Inauguration of Tutankhamun's replica tomb, 30th April 2014

tion of 2011 numbers have dropped markedly. For those that do still come, a visit to Tutankhamun's tomb is a must, just as it has been ever since it was first discovered in 1922. But for nearly a hundred years a constant stream of visitors breathing out hot, moist air has begun to damage the delicate murals and threaten them with mould. The curators of the cave paintings at Lascaux had exactly the same problem. They solved it by building a completely accurate and perfectly detailed facsimile of the original cave.

Now Egypt has come up with the same solution and has just opened a facsimile of Tutankhamun's tomb, its creation and installation supervised by Adrian Lowe, a British artist and master restorer. He hopes the life size facsimile will provide as good an experience as the original and says

"What I hope you'll be able to see is that it's possible to create an exact copy that from a normal viewing distance looks exactly like the tomb. And more than that – actually feels like a tomb."

All images in this book are copyright and have been provided courtesy of the following:

WIKICOMMONS
commons.wikimedia.org

Hopkins in Egypt Today, Tumblr, Crystalinks, SAFF, Trustees of British Museum, Associated Press

Acknowledgements:

Wikipedia

Chronicle of the Pharaohs - Peter A. Clayton
Thames & Hudson Ltd 2006

The Murder of Tutankhamun - Bob Brier
Weidenfeld & Nicholson 1998

Temples, Tombs & Hieroglyphs - Barbara Mertz
Brockhampton Press 1999

Design & Artwork: ALEX YOUNG

Published by: DEMAND MEDIA LIMITED

Publisher: JASON FENWICK

Written by: IAN MACKENZIE